AF539333

Value Education in Global Perspective

Published by :
Lotus Press Publishers & Distributors

Introduction

The most serious problem that is being faced by our society today is the rapid degradation of our cultural heritage which is the mirror of our values, morals and customs etc. The present condition of our society is changing rapidly with new innovations in technologies and modern means of communication. Every individual is in cut throat competition and material achievement has transformed the human being to a mechanical robot. Status and good salary package are the two factors on which the rate of success of an individual is assessed. But if this is so then why is it that even after achieving these goals people are still frustrated and unhappy? Why are people with high status and position in society hunting for mental peace? The answer to these questions may be within our inner soul. If we look our past, today there is a total crisis of values. It is really surprising that a country which was acknowledged by the world as the custodian of moral and spiritual ethics, where a king like Harischandra sacrificed his wife and sons for truth, is facing problems like terrorism. The accusation of the ills of society like embezzlement of public fund, molestation, robbery and corruption has been labelled on the growth of population. However, these are only excuses to console ourselves. In India there has been a rapid erosion of social, moral, cultural and political values. In the race of competition, we have forgotten our rich socio-cultural heritage. We have become indifferent towards our families. Joint families have segregated and most of the population has started confining themselves into their narrow territory. If required we are ready to win the race at the cost of our motherland. People have become reluctant to performing their duties towards their families. In recent studies it has been found that most of the people are acquainted with their fundamental rights but not their duties. Rights and duties are two sides of the same coin. It is quite obvious that one cannot be achieved without achieving the other.

Hence, today in our education system the curriculum should be framed in such a way that will help our young generation inculcate values which can save them from the darkness of self centeredness, unlimited greed, bribery, corruption, violence, distortions, frustration etc. It has also become necessary to give a proper thrust to our education system which will be able to focus on all round development of an individual.

In the present day scenario the curriculum of schools and colleges is mainly centered on superficial and material benefits rather than inner and psychological development. The fantasy and the purity of the mind of a child is distorted badly by our so called classroom education where the teachers are always under pressure to complete the syllabus but very little thought is given to the mental growth of the child. Classrooms are more or less a battle field where every parent and their ward are busy in winning the race by simply acquiring and vommiting the information (knowledge). Unfortunately in this rat race, students lag behind, develop complexes which ultimately pushes them to a corner characterized by negativity and poor personality development. The education system should not be packed with dry, boring information only. It should provide the students avenues to inculcate social, spiritual and moral values. Prof. Kreet Joshi truly emphasized value education with following words:

"In fact value education is overdue and we feel that appropriate measures should have been taken soon after attainment of independence."

The erosion of values is now a national phenomenon— complex and gigantic. The task of national development is massive and comprehensive. No worth while achievement is possible without an upsurge of ethical values, of cleanliness of public life instead of the prevailing cynicism and corruption. The National Commission (1964-66), strongly recommended that a serious defect in the school curriculum is the absence of social, moral and spiritual values. A national system of education aimed towards life, needs and aspiration of the people cannot afford to ignore this purposeful force. The conscious and organized attempts should be made in the process of education. Required steps should be taken to include the topics to pave the way for inculcation of social, cultural and the spiritual values.

This book is written in the hope that inculcation of moral, ethical, social, cultural and spiritual values among the student of schools and colleges will gain some importance. I believe all those who are sensitive towards education and values will get their ideas on the topics synthesized through this volume.

I am thankful to my guide, friend and philosopher Prof. K. K. Jain without whose blessings this endeavour would not come in this shape. I am also very thankful to Prof. L.C. Singh Ex. Head, Deptt of Tr. Education NCERT, New Delhi. I am also thankful to Prof. B. S. Dagar former Head of the Dept. MSI & Director, Dr. M. S. Choudhary for taking keen interest in the theme. I am thankful to my B.Ed. student Sabri Ghosh for her editing support. I must thank all those known and unknown authors whom I have quoted without their prior permission. I should not forget the support of my wife Jyotsna, dear daughter Kritika and sweet son Shreyas who are my source of inspiration. I should record my thanks and appreciation to Sh. A. S. Sehgal, Director, Lotus Press and his enthusiastic associates who could bring out the book with an impressive get-up in a record time.

Dr. Dhananjay Joshi

Contents

Chapter-1
Importance of Value Education

Introduction

The behaviour of any person is a reflection of his values, valueless life is meaningless. Society and environment have a unique role in the formation of values since human beings cannot live without society. In this regard famous scholar Emile Durkhem is of the opinion, "Impact of society is fully reflected in the personality of a human being." This inner and outer behaviour reflects social consciousness of the society. Therefore, many thinkers have termed society as a moral power. Moral and spiritual development is considered a very important part of the curriculum for students. Probably it is more important than the whole of material development. Moral and spiritual development is the main function of those human values without which no other social function is possible. In fact, without value education process itself will become meaningless and irrelevant. In reflection to value education the Supreme Court in its historical judgement given on 12th September 2002, said that value based education has become the need of the hour.

The great philosopher Plato defined education as training which develops good morality in the children through good habits. In the words of father of the nation Mahatma Gandhi—the whole function of education can be expressed in one word i.e. morality. It means morality and moral education are key elements without which education remains incomplete. Today the world is progressing at the speed at which moral values are declining. The whole world has established many standards but the world has created many *'Bhasmasur'* for the whole of mankind like atom bombs, environment crisis, terrorism, violence and malice etc. By and large today mankind is at the gun point of destructive powers. Fundamental values like good-will, tolerance, honesty, simplicity, cleanliness are fighting the aforesaid crisis. In this regard, the great philosopher Ross says that if we want to construct a high class civilization through education and maintain it and want to protect it from decline, then education must be based on morality. This implies that if we develop other human aspects which are removed from morality, the effects would be harmful, for example if science and technology are used by the educated class without a moral base say for destructive aims. Perhaps illiteracy would be better than education.

Need of Moral Values

The ancient Indian scholars assumed that mere intellectual achievement has no importance if they lack proper urge and character. In their view the only important thing was good behaviour. It implies that good behaviour was supreme religion for them.

"Aachar parmo dharm shrutyupta smriti aevch"

It is mentioned in *Manusmriti* that if a person is less knowledgeful, but virtuous, then he is better than an immoral but knowledgeful person.

"Savitrimatrasaropi varam vipra suyatrantit,
Nayantrit tartrivedoapi sarvanshi sarvavikrya"

In fact, if education cannot provide students the training of analysing and taking decisions wisely about the future problems, then it is disregarding one of its important purposes. Four pursuits of values have been prescribed in ancient Indian culture viz. religion, wealth, lust and salvation. Religion is a very practical and important value in the view of social context. Religion itself is an accumulation of innumerable virtues which can be stated as follows:

"Dhriti shama damoteyam shochmindriyaniqrahe
Dhirvidhya satyam krodha dashkam dharam lakshanam."

It means patience, forgiveness abstainment from stealing, pride, virtuousity, self restraint, wisdom, truth, and control over anger are the main traits of the religion. In the epic *Mahabharata's* Shanti Parva, it is clearly mentioned that the gist of Sanatan Dharam is that man speaks truth, gives charity, carries out aesthetic practices, follows virtousity, has satisfaction etc. It is also mentioned in *Mahabharata* that noble people do not guide any creature through *man, karam, vani* but shows kindness and the feeling of giving everyone one thing or the other and sum it as the nature of noble soul and good behaviour. Gandhiji believed that truth, non-violence, *satyagraha,* celibacy and not hearing or seeing evil are the supreme moral values. He had firm faith in *vaishnavjan* (people of God Vishnu) and *'Vaishnavageet'* (song of Vishnu) and used to sing the following geet in his prayer.

"Vaishnavjan to tenne kahiya, je peer parai janne re,
Par dukhe upkar kare, tore man abhiman na anne re"

In Buddhism, the message of moral values is written in *Ashtang Marg.* In Jainism non-violence, not giving anyone trouble, the policy of live and let live, peace, fraternity, good-behaviour, vegetarianism etc. are basic values. Christianity also accepts truth, non-violence, brotherhood, forgiveness, beneficence, etc. and presents the presumption of a peaceful society. Islam also gives the message of equality and brotherhood. Each and every religion of the world has accepted universal moral values as the base of human world.

Actually, the development of moral and social values should have been inculcated in education, but in present circumstances it is nowhere to be found.

Gurudev Ravindra Nath Tagore once said "We were busy in decorating the cage till now but the bird of the cage is still hungry." This fact is true even after so many years. Dr. Zakir Hussein was of the opinion that we should not sacrifice morality for technical progress, rather this progress should be presented in such a way that it may become a means of strengthening high human-values. In the wake of decline of moral values and civic-sense, high rate of crime, decline in restraints, the famous Urdu poet has said:

"Sabhi kuch ho raha hain is tarakee ke zamane mein,
Magar ye kya gazab hein aadami insan nahi hota"

In this regard, the great scientist of the 20th century, Einstein opines that time is the most difficult for a school when it has to resort to fear, terror and show of difficult power. Such type of behaviour hurts students. The emotions and confidence are destroyed. In such an environment students will become cowards. However, work has a goal in the schools and in life as well—feeling of happiness in doing work and its results and knowledge of value towards the society and their usefulness. Turning human-beings into experts is not enough. Education must make them useful machines. Education today is unable to give human beings balanced development of personality. Knowledge of value and life, and development of sensibility are must for the students. Students should adopt the vastness of beauty and the base of morality. Otherwise such expertise will put them into the category of trained animals in place of providing a balanced personality. In this regard the National Education Commission (1964-66) has also accepted that the lack of proper social, moral and spiritual values in the school syllabus as a major drawback.

The Concept of Values

Let us try to understand the meaning of the term 'value'. According to Prof. R. C. Das "A value may be defined as something which you consider very dear, which you strive to acquire, preserve or protect and about which you can think and make judgement about the alternates of action available in a situation in relation to the value."

John Dewey's (1939) concept of values include:

1. The idea of prizing, cherishing and holding dear.
2. The idea of reflection and making connections between the factors of the situation in one's existence to the end that intelligence is employed and that improved judgement is concluded.
3. The idea that action in support of an approved value will be taken.

Thus a value has three aspects: an affective or emotional aspect, a cognitive or thinking aspect and a psychomotor or doing aspect. One feels strongly about a value, can think of alternatives of action that support a value and would like to take action to uphold the value.

There are different kinds of values which people acquire and support to different degrees and the value profile of one person differs from the value profile of another person. Values have been classified in various ways and tests have been constructed to measure the relative ranking given to these values by a person.

Theories of Classification of Values

Western scholars have described several ethical theories. The main theories to judge the act of a man are as below:-

1. ***Hedonistic Theory***: In this theory pleasure is the base. Human words and deeds are termed as good or bad on this very basis.
2. ***Intuitional Theory***: In this theory intuition is taken

as standard instead of pleasure. Man's act is judged by intuition only.

3. ***Rigorist Theory***: In this theory neither pleasure nor intuition but duty is the sole standard. This theory emphasises objectivity and rationalism and has no place for emotion. According to this theory duty is the supreme concern and no other worldly matters.
4. ***Legalistic Theory***: According to this theory the authority of law of the land is the supreme. Morality is equated with leading of life according to the law only.
5. ***Idealistic Theory***: According to this theory perfection is the only standard. Any personality or idea is termed as good, if it is perfect. There may be several measures for rating the perfection.
6. ***Religious Theory***: According to this theory religion is the standard, which binds a group, a community etc. It (religion) may be revealed or natural. Revealed religion is the one, which is governed by various supreme personalities (saviours) like Lord Rama, Krishna, Christ, Buddha, Mahavira etc. Natural religion is based on several compassions governing the human behaviour through a very broad spectrum. In the context of 'value education' natural religion is to be preferred as it has a secular outlook, a vital requirement of our educational system.

Value Education intended for desired modifications in the individual's (students) behavioural patterns apparently involves four factors— society, environment, individual and school. Individual's personality is projected as good or bad as a result of his /her interaction with society, environment and school synchronically. Environment and school together

Value Education in Global Perspective

Dr. Dhananjay Joshi

4735/22, Prakash Deep Building
Ansari Road, Darya Ganj,
New Delhi - 110002

Lotus Press : Publishers & Distributors
Unit No. 220, 2nd Floor, 4735/22, Prakash Deep Building,
Ansari Road, Darya Ganj, New Delhi- 110002
Ph.: 23280047, 98118-38000
• E-mail : lotuspress1984@gmail.com
www.lotuspress.co.in

Value Education in Global Perspective

ISBN: 81-8382-007-7

Printed & Published by : **Lotus Press Publishers & Distributors,** New Delhi-02

Dedicated to

my

Parents

play a very significant role in building the personality of the individual because values grow from our purposes, aspirations, beliefs, attitudes, feelings, interests, convictions etc. that have close link with the society and environment around us.

The term value is a complex term. There is no consensus among scholars like Macmillan, Kneller, Superka, Ahrens and so on for its definition. This is such a pivotal term that each school of thought invests the word with its own definition. In the Indian perspective it can be roughly said that the term 'virtue' is the nearest, if not identical to the term 'value'. In our scriptures the terms like non-violence (*Ahimsa*), truthfulness, purity, spiritual wisdom, self-discipline, piety, friendliness, charity, devotion to duty etc. are called virtues. These and other similar terms are termed as 'value' by the Western psychologists and philosophers. These are traditional values inherited from past. In order to match the emerging aspirations and needs of the changing society many fresh values are also involved, which will be explained through the lines to follow.

Need of Value based Education

The need for Value based Education cannot be over-emphasised particularly in the present setup of the society. According to Dr. J.E. Adamson the Individual and the Environment, "We have education treated in relation to three worlds that make up his complete environment—the educational, the social world, and the moral world. Obviously all the natural and physical sciences belong to the first, all the humanist studies to the second and all the ethical and religious to the third. Our educationists have spent lot of ink in formalizing the curriculum regarding the natural and social world but very little has been brought about for the third, the most subtle world—the moral world. There have been a lot of controversies about the separation of religion from the state. In order to make our system of education more and more secular in nature, the moral upliftment of the child has been neglected. Since the last few decades, the western world has taken it up as a challenge and devised several ways and methods for cultivating moral and spiritual values in the minds of the students. We also come across a sort of syllabus for Moral Education. But in our society the awakening in this direction has been too late. Till recently there was substantial move."

In May, 1981, a high level seminar on Moral Education was held at Shimla. On the recommendations of this seminar there was a move to form a syllabus for value-oriented education for different classes: but it has not yet been finalised so far because of several socio-cultural constraints. The Education Commission, 1964-66 headed by Prof. D.S. Kothari had very rightly observed:

"A serious defect in the school curriculum is the absence of provision for education in social, moral and spiritual values. In the life of the majority of Indians, religion is a great motivating force and is intimately bound up with the formation of character and inculcation of ethical values. A national system of education that is related to the life, needs and aspirations of the people cannot afford to ignore this purposeful force. We recommend, therefore, that conscious and organized attempts be made for imparting education in social, moral and spiritual values with the help, wherever possible, of the ethical teaching of great religions."

From the reports of several committees and commissions appointed from time to time it is obvious that there has been consensus of opinion regarding inclusion of values in educational system. This is the high time to do so, if we intend to safeguard the present set-up of society from further deterioration and degeneration.

The resolution adopted at Wardha Conference(1937) does

not contain any reference to moral and religious education. When Mahatma Gandhi was asked about this he remarked very aptly—"We have left out the teaching from Wardha Scheme of education because we are afraid that religions as they are taught and practised today lead to conflict rather than unity. But on the other hand, I hold that the truths that are common to all religions can and should be taught to all children, these truths cannot be taught through words or through books— the children can learn these truths only through daily life of the teacher. If the teacher lives up to the tenets of truth and justice then only can children learn that 'Truth and Justice are basis of all religions'

Thus, we may firmly conclude that there has been a consensus of opinion regarding the teaching of moral and spiritual values but the main setback is the present social setup itself, in which positive teacher-taught interaction does not seem to be up to the mark. That is why inspite of several well thought of resolutions and recommendations of so many commissions and committees we have not been able to introduce 'Value Based Education', in our schools and colleges. It should be emphasized again and again that value education is the need of the hour.

Objectives of Value Education

The main aim of value-oriented education is to make the students good citizens who may share their responsibilities in the changing set-up of the society in order to give the desired shape and image to the society and the country at large. The following can be enumerated as the general objectives of moral education for the school stage:

1. To promote in children such basis and fundamental qualities as truthfulness, cooperation, love and compassion, peace and non-violence, courage, equality, justice, dignity of labour, common brotherhood of man and scientific temper.

2. To train children to become responsible citizens in their personal and social lives.
3. To enable them to understand and appreciate the national goals of socialism and democracy and to contribute to their realization.
4. To create in them an awareness of the socio-economic conditions and to motivate them to improve the same.
5. To enable them to become open and considerate in their thought and behaviour and rise above prejudices based on religion, language, caste or sex.
6. To help them understand and appreciate themselves and continually strive for their inner development and thus moving towards the goal of self actualization; and
7. To develop in them proper attitudes:
   a) Towards oneself and fellow beings.
   b) Towards one's own country.
   c) Towards people of other countries leading to international understanding.
   d) Towards life and environment, and
   e) Towards all religions.

Development of Moral-Values

The development of knowledge and values starts immediately in the process of socialisation. Teaching like prohibition of telling lies and stealing are given in their childhood. Primary moral-values education is different from the development of values in adults.

Many psychologist believe that the process of reinforcement creates a sense of reward or punishment. Teachers teach small children to differentiate between right and wrong. This process keeps going on continuously. They are satisfied with just imposing pseudeo-morality on the child who is taken for granted later. Ultimately, he has to accept actual moral-values to enable all-round development of personality.

A teenager is unable to develop value system on his own values even if he wants to create such a system. Experienced fundamentalists believe that a person should at least have ability enough to take decisions according to his prudence (what is actual philosophy of moral-values, Generally a five or ten year old child does not have enough moral ability to lay out principles on his own.

It is necessary to discuss all the possible options. Children should have the ability to discuss effective logic, possibility and planning. But the ability of discussion on the importance and effeicacy of planning options does not develop during teenage or even after this stage and sometimes it is not developed in any stage at all.

Principles of Development of Moral-Values

Morality and its development has been a psychological thought for centuries. The development of moral values is related to the process by which children are able to differentiate between right and wrong, good or bad etc. The special focus of research in the development of moral values is the development of moral prudence and character.

Moral knowledge includes the principle of learning, moral result, blandishment, behaviour of children and how they adopt. Moral character, situational necessity, ethics, related activity shows actual behaviour.Following psycologist has given principles of Moral Development.

1. Piaget

Piaget expounded his principle of moral development by asking children questions based on short stories and hearing their logic. According to him, morality was social rule, equality and justice for all. He found that children are affected by the imposition of social rule, and parents' behaviour. Feeling of justice is developed in children from social experiences. Piaget discovered two stages of moral development in children of 4-12 years of age. The first or elementary stage—the heteronomous morality or external morality i.e. following the moral values suggested by others as seen in children of 4-7 age. The second stage was self-control morality or internal morality found in 10-12 years of age. In this stage the child develops and obeys the internal moral values.

2. Kalburg Larenz

He expounded principles of moral developments on the basis of the examining the answers which he gave to the children, teenagers and youth to solve their moral problems.

First Level: Prior to Morality

Moral-values are seen in outer, partly physical activity and wrong deeds. A child is responsible for the value and regulations and analysis the established standard. This level has two stages. The first stage is obedience and punishment oriented which protects us from the things related to more power or reputation or problem solving. The second stage is undeceitful egoism which fulfils mechanically one's own needs and each others needs. There is awareness of relativism of values of one another's needs.

Second level: Confirmation of Introduction

At this stage, only moral values are inclined in performing right work, organising traditional process and others ambitions.

Third level: Self Accepted Moral Principles

Morality has been defined as the confirmation of divided

human rights or responsibility with favourable privileges. The level is based on the confirmation of the level, internal determination of doing a work, decision of right or wrong and inner thought process.

Principle and Discernment

Morality is not only based on a permanent law but also based on discernment as a directive agent which pressurizes us to do the work without being affected by other activities in our environment.

Bandra and Walter

Bandra expounded a social behaviour approach for the social activities, socialisation and development of personal principles. He said that moral development and decision can be clearly understood through the performance of agents of socialisation. According to him, suitable sample shows adaptability in different conditions of moral behaviour.

Karl Roger

Teenage is the right time for possible development of personal values. It is the time when a child learns to be self-dependent. He believes in himself at this stage and develops his moral values and becomes capable enough to take decisions regarding what is right or wrong. Rogers expounded three stages of development of matured value system.

Values and their Sources[1]

Accordung to father Kunnakal these values are the result of the standards set by various religions. It is therefore, necessary for us to interpret the term 'secular' enshrined in our Constitution correctly. The term should mean a system wherein equal respect is shown to all the religions. It should

1. *Father Kunnakal (Honb' Arch Bishop) Journal of Value Education published by NCERT*

not be construed to mean absence of religion nor advocating an irreligious society. Even though no state patronage for any one religion is implied or intended, there is no escape from imparting religious teaching in essence, though not in name. We have to bear in mind that these values and principles have their source in the scriptures and the sayings of seers and sages, who have been religious leaders of historical importance. Whereas love, care and compassion top the list of these values, truth, non-injury and universal brotherhood are the pillars of this edifice.

We in India may be concerned with only a few of the major religions of the world yet it would be appropriate to see what are the basic tenets of all of them. The oldest of the major global religions which developed in the West, is Judaism. The Bible of this faith is written in Hebrew and is called Torah. It contains laws governing many aspects of life. It says, "You shall love your Lord, your God with all your heart, with all your soul and with all your might."

Next comes Christianity, which also advocates love. The Sermon on the Mount says: "Love your enemies, do good to those who hate you, bless those who curse you, pray for those who treat you spitefully. Treat others, as you would like them to treat you. If you love only those who love you, what credit is that to you? Even sinners love those who love them. Islam is well known for its social laws based on institutionalized customs. These are derived from the life of the Prophet. These are based on five pillars of faith or *'Imaan'*, prayer or *'Salaat'*, fasting or *'Sawm'*, alms-giving or *'Zakaat'* and pilgrimage or *'Haj'*. Put in a more detailed way, these are as follows:

1. Profession of the oneness of God and the messengership of Muhammad called *'Dawa'*.

2. Five daily prayers called *'Nimaz'*.
3. Fasting during the holy month of Ramazan called *'Sawm'*.
4. Giving in charity at least 2.5 per cent of one's income called *'Zakat'*.
5. Pilgrimage to the holy city of Mecca called *'Haj'*.

If the religious aspect of these tenets is set aside, it will be seen that they teach us submission, obedience, charity, compassion and discipline. Buddhism shows us the eightfold path of right view, right aspiration, right speech, right behaviour, right livelihood, right effort, right thoughts and right contemplation. Jainism teaches us truth and non-injury. In Hindu tradition the scriptures are full of moral and ethical values. The code of Manu lays down social laws and requires sacrifice of individual desire for the sake of order in the society. Patanjali's yoga prescribes, among other things, two sets of rules: 'Yams' that we should not do like killing, stealing, lying, etc. and 'Niyama'— that we ought to do like being modest, living with simplicity, being tolerant, being sincere and maintaining mental and physical hygiene.

If these common tenets of the prominent world religions are incorporated in the educational system we shall not only be producing good citizens, but also combating the forces of exclusivism, racism, fundamentalism and the political use of religious identity.

Professor Timothy Miller, a specialist in new religious movements says about human culture that "...it is always evolving, it is always reinventing its own past and present anything truly new under the Sun could arise". He has categorized world religions into three groups. The first group he calls the religions of the Pre-Axial age. The Hindu Sanatana Dharma primarily represents this age. It sees this world as suffused with the sacred. The second group belongs to the Axial age between eighth and fifth century BC. This group includes Buddha, Confucius, Zorostra, Jewish Prophets and the Greek philosophers. These drew a sharp distinction between the worldly reality and the transcendent invisible reality. The third group belongs to Post-Axial period and includes Christianity and Islam. These religions continued and developed the theme of the religions and thinkers of the Axial period. The central ethical teachings of all these were, however, similar if not identical. "Treat others as you would like them to treat you. Do nothing unto others that would cause you pain, if it were done to you." This universal message of human behaviour is conveyed by the *Mahabarata* (5.1.517), Lord Mahavira, Buddha (Udana-varga 5.18), Analects of Confucius (15.23), Zoroastra, Judaism, Talmud Shabbat (31a), Christianity (Mathew 7.12). Islam (sunnah) as also Guru Granth Sahib (259) as recorded in the compilation of the *Temple of Understanding*. This forces us to conclude that the symbols of different religions may be different, the message of universal love and universal brotherhood is common among them all.

The *Vedas* have conceived of a harmonious world order by declaring *Vasudhaiva kutumbakam* the world is but one family. They have visualized a protected and safe haven for the entire mankind by saying *Yatra vishvam bhavati eka needam*—where the entire world becomes a nest to give shelter to all. The *Bhagavad Gita* has also summed up the desirable qualities of an ideal person in the first three *shlokas* of Chapter XVI. These include fearlessness, purity of heart, charity, altruism, non-injury, truth, compassion, modesty, forgiveness, absence of hatred and anger. If our children develop these qualities from the beginning, imagine what an ideal character and personality our future generation will have. It will, therefore, do a lot of good to our nation and to the mankind at large if these values are incorporated suitably in the educational system in a systematic way and at the appropriate levels.

Modern View about Values[2]

John Heenan, has traced the concept of values to Nietszche. He writes:

"The change came in 1880's when the German philosopher, Friedrich Nietzsche began to speak of values as moral beliefs and attitudes. Nietzsche used the word Values consciously, repeatedly and insistently to signify what he took to be the most profound event in history. His transvaluation of values was to be the final, ultimate revolution against both classical and Judaic-Christian ethics. Nietzsche believed that with their death would come the death of truth and above all any morality. There would be no good or evil, no virtue or vice but only values that were personal and subjective. Then, at last, Nietzsche believed humanity would be freed from the prison of virtues and morality. Over the years Nietzche's concept of values was absorbed unconsciously and without resistance into the ethos of modern society. With the growing use of the word values, the word virtues, those traits of character that aspire to moral excellence like honesty, compassion, courage and perseverance, fell into disuse. But contrary to Nietzsche's belief and hope, virtues did not die but became to be regarded as moral or objective core values. For this reason, today, any list of values is likely to include in the old virtues. Values, as we know them, can be either preferences or principles, which represent the opposite ends of the moral spectrum. Preference values are something to have while values that are principles are something to be. What this philosopher did not understand was that virtues, moral or objective core values, worked in three interrelated parts: moral knowing, moral feeling and moral behaviour that connect to good character."

2. *John Heenan, Director New Zealand Foundation for Value Education.*

In fact good character is the habit of knowing the good, the habit of desiring the good and the habit of doing the good. The teaching of core values of honesty, kindness, compassion, respect and responsibility by parents and schools is essential if we have to restore and advance our social cohesion. Education has two main goals: to master the skills of literacy and to build good character. To create a society of good citizens, we must have education for character and intellect, for decency and literacy, and for virtue and skills and efficiency. The New Zealand Foundation for Value Education has made the following observations, which are worth noting.

"In a Danish understanding of value education there are two central concepts: spirits and life's ability. Spirits implies an elementary experience of life's meaning, fulness and life's ability implies a content of leisure ability, family ability and political ability, with a definite meaning, wish and ability to take responsibility for your own life. Logstrup (1985) coined the phrase 'life understanding' which means to give priority to children's experience of identity building and self-esteem. Value education primarily is an ethical subject, if ethics is defined as follows: A vision about the good life together with and for other people. In Danish literature it is common to distinguish between morals, ethics and values. "Morals are standards for identifying right and wrong. Ethics is the theory about what is right and what is wrong. Value indicates a firm conviction that a particular behaviour or kind of life is personally or socially preferred."

Secularism and the Values

Some thinkers have treated advocating of values as an effort to the lessons of morality taught by the traditional religions. They have considered it as an aspect of secularization of the society. In his book on 'Sufism' William Stoddart has expressed his views in these words:

"Modern civilization has its routes in the Renaissance, that great inrush of secularization, when nominalism vanquished realism, individualism (or humanism) replaced universalism, and empiricism banished scholasticism. The principles lying behind the genesis and nature of modern civilization were lucidly set forth in a remarkable series of works, published in the earlier part of this century, by Rene Guenon, who was also a masterly exponent of the metaphysics and symbolism of all the religions. And even a richer and more far-reaching exposition of religion and metaphysics (coupled with a penetrating critique of modern civilization) has come in the second part of this century, from Frithj of Schuon. The same principle was brilliantly represented in the English-speaking world in the later writings of Ananda Coomaraswamy. Among other things these authors demonstrated that there is a perfect spiritual equivalence between pre-renaissance (or Medieval) Christianity and the various oriental religions."

Such misgivings may not be well placed, for the human mind cannot remain static. Its thinking is evolutionary in character and once the thinking changes, the environment of the society changes. The fact, however remains that the links with the past and with the roots cannot altogether be severed. What is today called 'human values' incorporates all that till yesterday was termed as religious morality and ethics. There is no gain saying the fact that there is a paramount need to make values the essential ingredient of the educational framework. It has to be understood that by demolishing the old set-up in the name of secularization we shall create an undesirable vacuum. It is, therefore, necessary that the void so created is filled with a new set-up, with due regard to the present day needs and an eye towards building a glorious future for the mankind.

Religious Instruction Vs. Value Education

In Wardha Scheme[3] moral and religious education were

not included for fear that it may lead to conflicts rather than unity. This fear was not baseless. Though the Constitutional guarantee of religious freedom exists but the operation of instructions from a particular religion is likely to lead to controversy and conflicts.

India is a vast country with many different religions. Each religion has something to give to us. Tolerant attitude in religious matters has been one of the most prominent features of our composite culture. Many races have found pleasant refuge on our land. The scriptures of different creeds—the *Bible*, the *Quoran*, the *Upanishads*, the *Zandavesta*— appear different but their goal is one and the same i.e., to establish the brotherhood of man and to bring about peace and harmony in the society.

Therefore, values like nationalism, national integration, patriotism, respect for other religion etc. should attract our attention with an emphasis on suitable practical line of actions.

According to Vivekanand three things are necessary to make every man great, every nation great:

1. Conviction of the powers of goodness
2. Absence of jealousy and suspicion
3. Helping all who are trying to be good and do good

These days parents also come across with conflicting ideologies. At times there is utter lack of clarification of Values. From time to time they have orientation in values through good reading, listenning to discourses of socio-religious leaders, discussions with their friends etc. The students get their first lesson in values like truthfulness, charity, concern for other, kindness to birds and animals, honesty, obedience etc. at home. Therefore, values must be

3. *Wardha Scheme also known as Basic Education 1937, promoted by Mahatma Gandhi.*

clear to the parents. Then only can we hope for their right and apt inculcation or internalization.

Paradigm of Values

Clarification of *different* values at *different* levels for persons from *different* strata of the society is very essential. In the traditional terminology of virtue (*dharma*) and sin and through different situations these values can be well clarified. Our spiritual leaders and social reformers have been doing this through their speeches, writings etc. for example we may go through the following words of Swami Vivekanand[4].

"Doing good to others is virtue (dharma): injuring others is sin. Strength and manliness are virtue; weakness and cowardice are sin. Independence is virtue; dependence is sin. Loving others is virtue; hating others is sin. Faith in God and one's own self is virtue; doubt is sin. Knowledge of oneness is virtue; seeing diversity is sin."

Clarity in values alone can satisfy the individuals and stand to the test of utility in their social life. If it is not materialized students' restlessness will be brooming constantly to the deliterious extent. For national integration, clarification of values should be taken as continuous programme. It should be through various mural and intramural activities. The best of our traditional (ancient) values should be brought about and students should be exposed to them through several situations.

On different occasions Swami Budhanand has emphasized the need of well defined values for national unity:

"In today's India, the scene that presents itself before any impartial observer is a matter of conflicting ideologies amidst drift and restlessness. The ancient values, which had once given to the nation strength and hope, have been

4. *Swami Vivekannad in his complete work on real vedant published by Ramakrishan math.*

pushed into the background, and many new ideas are contending to fill the gap. Thus there is a quest for well-defined values. Satisfying the aspirations of all. In such a situation, the youth of the country are restive."

Value-orientation aims at modification of behaviour, which may be treated as different from psychological behaviourism because it would not work in the context of value education. In this context, two approaches are important—(1) value clarification and (2) Moral development stage theory or, as Lawrence Kohlberg its propounder would put it, the cognitive—developmental approach. These two approaches have attracted the attention of educators as these approaches offer solutions to meta ethical relativism and pluralism. Generally educators are confronted with these twin problems. According to Kohlberg "A more differentiated and integrated moral structure handles more moral problems, conflicts of view in a more stable or self-consistant way. Because conventional morality is not fully universal and prescriptive, it leads to continual self-contradiction, to definitions of right which are different for Republicans and Democrats, for Americans and Vietnamees, for fathers and sons."

Therefore, right or wrong action should be defined in terms of their conditioning by the environment (students, teachers, peer-groups, community etc.) and their consistence with one's cultural value tenets. As far as possible indoctrination should be avoided.

Self-discipline

The body of modern society seems to be lacking in self-discipline. Self-discipline is, in fact, the basis of all values which not only moulds the individual's character, but also determines his reactions and responses to other values and society at large. Self-discipline is the maintenance of orderliness and obedience with regard to the self and one's conscience. It takes into account various spheres of one's conduct and style of life, like respect for values such as truth, punctuality, responsibility, adjustment, devotion for duty, faith or trust in others, care and concern for others and their feelings and devotion to one's aims and objectives or fulfilment of one's duty. Thus, indiscipline of the self and of one's individuality can be called the main crisis of values that has hit our society. The crying need of modern society is to inculcate the spirit of self-discipline and the values that follows from it in every individual from his childhood through proper education and training.

It is widely believed that the modernization process is responsible for the crisis in values to a large extent. The reasons are not far to seek. Modernization involves industrialization, use of modern and advanced techniques in agriculture and all other spheres of life and work. With modernization comes better communication that bridges the gap not only between places but also between people. The result is that the traditional values of a small closely knit society which demands cooperation, loyalty, dependence on relations, neighbours get eroded and people tend to ignore these values. They become more self-reliant and more impersonal in their conduct. Had the modern society consciously tried to retain or imbibe the values of self-discipline in individuals, the crisis of valuc that is so widespread could have been contained. Self-discipline teaches one not only to value one's rights but to respect those of others equally.

The process of disintegration of values would soon prove to be disastrous, unless a conscious effort is made to reverse this trend and to inculcate in one and all, a spirit of self-discipline.

Educational Values

The values that the teachers are supposed to uphold,

cannot be delinked within the values that education, in general, is supposed to cherish. In the long history of mankind, education has always accomplished two major tasks:

a) To enable the younger generation to wrest from nature and shape according to requirements that which is needed by humanity for its survival and comfort, and

b) To mould the consciousness of the younger generation in such a manner that they would become useful and by and large satisfy members of the society to which they belong.

In terms of the first task, education, whether formal or informal, has taught the younger generation to become useful, productive members of the society, whether it be as an agriculturist, a potter, an astronomer, a modern scientist, a technocrat or a management expert. In the modern period, there has been great expansion in the educational system at all levels, particularly at the tertiary and the higher tertiary level to enable the young to become useful productive members of a highly scientific and technological society.

Coming to the second task, education again both formal and informal whether it is through the magic dances, stories, mythology or through the teaching of literature, social sciences, mass media etc. is an attempt to so mould the consciousness of the young that they will remain parts of the society and not revolt against it. It would do well to remember here that the educational system is a sub-system of the socio-cultural system and both affects the values of the system and is also affected by them.

In both the processes, whether turning out young people as useful productive units of society or in the process of building up their consciousness, certain values are perceptibly or imperceptibly inculcated in them and the education system of any country, in any age, becomes a vehicle for the transmission of values. These values can be values both for the preservation of an existing system or its transformation.

Role of Administration in Value Education

To facilitate this transformation in a constructive and revolutionary manner, the International Commission[5] on education pledged to undertake three major tasks:

A. Government should initiate a fundamental reshaping by national educational systems and participate in a global diagnosis of the education and training systems. The commission expresses the hope that national authorities will recognise the primordial necessity of placing educational problems in an over-all context, and seek answers to this all important question—does the educational apparatus, as now conceived, really satisfy the needs and aspirations of man and societies in our time?

B. National authorities should undertake a deeper scrutiny and understanding of the educational life of their societies and probe far beyond the previous trends of being mainly concerned with quantitative and qualitative aspect of education.

   In the past our main concern has been to do more than before and later on, better than before. We must now ask ourselves how to do different than before, because what was before is no longer suitable or relevant. Education is such a huge undertaking, it has so radical an influence on man's destiny, that it will be damaged if it is only considered in terms of structures, logistical means and processes. The very substance of education, its essential relationship to man and his

5. *International Commission on education also known as Delor's Commission (1996).*

development, its interaction with the environment as both product and factor of society must all be deeply scrutinized and extensively reconsidered.

C. National authorities should reshape their educational system on two parallel lines: (1) internal reforms and continued improvements of existing educational systems, and (2) search for innovative forms, for alternatives and fresh resources.

Indeed, the most significant change in the world of education should be the advent of democracy which will be living, creative and evolving. For this to be achieved, social structures must be changed and the privileges built into our cultural heritage must be reduced. Educational structures must be remodelled, to extend widely the field of choice and enable people to follow lifelong education patterns. Subject-matter must be individualized, pupils and students must be aware of their status their rights and their own wishes. Authoritarian forms of teaching must give away to relationship marked by independence, mutual responsibility and dialogue; pedagogical training must be geared to knowing and respecting the multiple aspect of human personality, guidance must replace selections, those making use of educational institutions must participate in their management and policy-making, the bureaucratic aspect of education must be broken down and its administration decentralized.

Such a programme of action obviously calls for a revolutionary transformation of the contemporary educational scenes everywhere.

Guidelines for Value based Education

Dr. Anil Vidhyalankar[6] has enumerated some basic principles for value Education. According to him these principles had been evolved as a result of the status study of moral education in Indian states and union territories conducted by NCERT, the joint study on Moral Education in Asian countries conducted by the National Institute of Educational Research, Tokyo, and a dialogue with a number of teachers and educational administrators and planners:

1. Moral Education should not be regarded as just another school subject.
2. Moral education is not education in religion.
3. There should be an integral approach in moral education.
4. Teaching of social responsibility should be the main aim of moral education.
5. Moral education cannot be separated from the socio-economic conditions prevailing in the society.
6. The atmosphere in the school influences moral development.
7. Instructions in moral education should be appropriate to the age-group of children.
8. Instructions in moral education should be problem-based.
9. All moral problems should be discussed frankly and sincerely.
10. No views should be imposed on children.
11. Moral education should have an integral practical part.
12. Moral education should be imparted in the context of the peculiar problems faced by the young people.
13. Moral education programme should be independent of ideologies and personalities.

6. *Dr. Anil Vidhyalendkar presented a paper at the High level conference on moral education at Shimla in may 1981.*

14. All teachers are teachers of moral education.
15. Nothing should be done in connection with moral education that would directly or indirectly induce immoral behaviour.
16. Moral education should have both compulsory and voluntary components.

Roles Recommended for Value and Character Development[1]

Role of the Teacher in Value Development

The emphasis on education for character development imposes on the teacher a very special responsibility. As character can best be imparted by the living example of the teacher, a high standard of ethics must become an indispensable part of the teaching profession. The country should demand that teachers themselves evolve high standards of self-discipline and ensure their implementation in their daily life, in their relationships with students, colleagues, and people in general, and in their professional performance.

Respect for teachers which had been emphasized in Indian culture, but which has been greatly eroded because of various factors, needs to be resurrected by various means including those which will provide high status and facilities to teachers.

New programmes of training will have to be formulated and implemented.

Considering that the teacher is the real bridge between the past and the future and carrier of cultural heritage from generation to generation, it must be expected from every

1. *Reference from National Agenda for Education (National Conference on Education) by Dharam Hinduja International Central Indic Research October-1997, New Delhi.*

teacher to become a perpetual student of the lessons of history and of the quest of the knowledge by the aid of which greater future can be built.

We speak today of the child-centred education, but only the teacher can really give concrete shape to this concept. For it is only the teacher who can introduce dynamic methods which would place the child in the centre of the learning process.

The role of the teacher will, in this context, be:

a) To observe his/her students, their inclinations and capacities, so as to be able to help them, with deep sympathy and understanding.

b) To become an animator rather than a mere lecturer, and to inspire much more than to instruct.

c) To aid students by processes of consultation and suggestion and develop in them the inner will to grow and progress.

It is the responsibility of the Government and of the people to provide to the teachers all the material and infrastructural facilities so that they can give all the time and energy to the progress and development of their students.

Pre-service training of teachers will require a thorough revision. If teachers are to ensure integral development of their students, they themselves have to be trained to attain higher and higher degrees of integration of their own personalities. Again, since there is an explosion of knowledge, teachers have to be trained in the art and science life-long education, in the art of learning to learn, and in the skills by which the advancing frontiers of knowledge can be brought nearer to their students.

Corresponding to the higher demands of training, the career graphs of teachers have to be critically revised, and both the government and the society have to bear the responsibility to provide to their teachers standards that are equivalent to a high quality of life.

Role of Students

While the educational system must provide all the necessary facilities, support and required atmosphere, it is upto the students themselves to make the right use of the aids provided to them. It is by their free will that they have to grow up into self-determining individuals striving constantly towards excellence, not in respect of studies, but also in respect of integral development of personality, physical, emotional, dynamic, intellectual, ethical, aesthetic and spiritual.

Students should gradually come to realize that self-knowledge and self-control constitute the most effective means of true self-fulfillment.

Teachers, parents and people in general would expect from the students that they will:

a) learn the secret of self-education, of learning to learn;

b) study and work widely and intensely, study and work with joy and application, progress constantly and thus learn how to remain perpetually youthful; and

c) become fearless and heroic in the quest of truth, harmony and liberty,

d) and work always at the boundaries of their limitations so as to surpass them by the constant aspiration to rise higher and higher.

Role of Parents

Parents are the first teachers of the children, and the pressure of our times imposes upon every parent to develop all that is expected of a good student and a good teacher.

Parents have to realize that the world is changing rapidly, that the horizons of knowledge are expanding constantly, and that children are growing in a new atmosphere of currents of culture in which the values of the East and the West blend. This creates a great deal of uncertainty and consequent disequilibrium. It is in these difficult times that parents have to build and maintain bonds of trust with children and guide them with love and understanding, with practical dexterity, and with largesse of mind and heart. They have to harmonise the demands of freedom with the demands of self-discipline.

Among all sections of the society, it is the parents who have perhaps the most difficult role. And it can be fulfilled by means of:

a) continuous programme of training;

b) participation in teachers-parents associations;

c) participation in their children's development processes;

d) deeper understanding of values of Indian culture and how they can be made active under the present difficult conditions where all that is good in the West is to be assimilated, and all that is injurious to our culture and its future has to be rejected; and

e) ensuring that children are protected from exposure to influences that are injurious to their value-oriented development.

A powerful parents movement requires to be launched in our country to undertake, encourage and support programmes that will enable them to discharge their difficult role.

There is a valuable suggestion that every parent whose child is enrolled in a school should be required to undergo an immediate programme of training, and as their children move forward, also they are required to undergo higher levels of training. This suggestion deserves to be implemented, and appropriate courses of training need to be devised and implemented.

Role of the Educational Administrator

The role of the educational administrator is bound to be even higher than that of anyone in this vital field of education. As captains of the educational domain, educational administrators have to be leaders, participants and servants rolled into one. They have to endeavour to guide parents, inspire teachers and serve the highest interests of the children. They also have to raise resources and employ them wisely and with utmost economy. They have to plan the future with boldness of an adventurer and meticulous skill of a goldsmith. They have to keep abreast of the educational developments nationally and globally, and they have to devise and employ various innovations by which the educational system remains vibrant with enthusiasm. Conferences, seminars, exhibitions, displays and cultural activities and various events have to be so organized that they would fill the atmosphere with vision and guidance, with joy, mirth and happiness.They also have to deal with mass media, and by means of various initiatives and programmes of action they have to ensure that these media subserve highest interests of education.

Role of Art in Education

A depressing aspect of our present system of education is that artistic abilities of our children are totally neglected or only marginally encouraged. The first aim of art education is purely aesthetic, the second is intellectual, and the third and the highest is spiritual. Music, art, and poetry may be viewed as a perfect education for the soul. When properly used they are the great educating, edifying and civilizing forces.

Young children with artistic talents should never experience lack of encouragement, facilities and opportunities to develop their talents and to express them; on the other hand, every child should be helped to enter into the domains of art and gain the capacity to understand and appreciate the uplifting role of art.

What is true of art is also true of craft and the educational system should cater to the children's potentialities to develop skills in respect of different crafts.

Role of Physical Education

An ancient Sanskrit adage declares—*sharira madyam khalu andharmasadhanam*—body is the means of fulfilment of dharma, i.e. every ideal which we can propose to ourselves and the law of its working out and its action.

Three important aspects of physical education must be emphasized in educational system: control and discipline of functions of the body; total methodical and harmonious development of all the parts and movements of the body; and rectification of deformities, if there are any.

Mystery and excellence of the human body should be underlined in the scheme of education so that students feel inspired to marvel at the wonder of body's complexities and remarkable machinery that has a natural impulse towards health and healing.

The neglect of physical education that has ruined our country's vigour and sense of discipline requires to be remedied with massive programmes of development of gymnasia, playgrounds, facilities for sports, combatives and aquatics. Physical education should not be looked upon as a pastime. It should be related to the ideal of healthy mind in a healthy body. Indispensable knowledge regarding physiology and hygiene, nutrition and proper dieting and useful skills related to first aid and helping oneself and others in situations of physical danger should be a part of physical education. Spirit of adventure should also be emphasized as a necessary part. Great qualities like those of sportsmanship, team spirit, practice of fair play, obedience to the decision of the referee or the umpire, acceptance of success and failure with grace and equanimity, and virtues of hardihood, endurance and perseverance can best be developed through well-planned programmes of physical culture. The nation where young men and women possess robust capacities of the physique, coupled with mental, ethical and aesthetic values can and will assurely rise higher and higher in providing leadership in all fields of life.

Role of National Spirit of Discipline

The country has regrettably paid minor attention to the creation of national spirit of discipline. Apart from rigorous physical education, there are various means by which this spirit can be generated and nourished. The role that scouts and guide movements can provide needs to be emphasized. N.C.C. and N.S.S. for which some facilities are provided at higher levels of school education and collegiate education, have remained in the periphery, and large majorities of our students remain indifferent to the requirements of national defence and qualities of discipline, heroism and courage remain depressed.

In several systems of education which are current in different parts of the world, students are obliged to have a compulsory period of training in the defence service of the country, and it is often suggested that every student in our country before getting certification for graduation, must be required to undergo similar training.

In the past, when such a proposal had come to be considered seriously at the governmental level, it was argued that the costs involved are extremely heavy and unbearable.

Today, when we see the course of indiscipline spreading in all sections of society, it seems rather imperative that our country should not only encourage scouts and guide movements but should also compel our students to participate compel in training where national spirit of discipline can be instilled. N.C.C., N.S.S. and some other equivalent programmes of sports and adventure should be offered, and with certification at the graduate level.

Contents of Education

A question is often asked as to what are the immediate yardsticks for determining what has to be called "quality education". The answer perhaps lies in the contents and methods of education that inspire every child to surpass his or her limitations, the quality of education attains its distinctiveness. Quality education promotes excellence amongst students, both individually and collectively.

The following aspects of contents of education will contribute to enhancing "quality education".

What Everyone Needs to Learn

If the Macaulian aim of education to produce clerks is to be effectively replaced by what Swami Vivekananda called "man making education", we have to conceive a new scheme of contents of learning. We have to provide for the essential knowledge that every individual needs to cultivate in order to become truly human and humane, irrespective of and in addition to one's own specialization. Since everyone possesses a physical body and a psychological complex of emotions, dynamism, thought and will, everyone needs to know the mystery and excellence of the human body, and how to harmonise demands of rationality, morality and aesthetic refinement. One also needs to learn how to practice power of concentration and a noble science and art of living. Everyone needs to be a good pupil and a good teacher, and everyone needs to learn how to grow into higher and deeper reaches of psychic and spiritual being. These and allied subjects need to be woven together in a graded manner so that they are brought to students effectively but in a very flexible manner throughout the living process of the growth of character and personality.

Vocational Education

Vocational education should be looked upon as an essential part of character development. The secret of vocation or profession lies in personality, and no personality is complete without the development of skills, in fact, vocational education needs to be so redesigned so that every student should have the possibility of at least two years' training in the skills suitable to a chosen vocation prior to any terminal point in the system of education, particularly prior to the end of elementary education.

Unfortunately, vocational education has still not become socially acceptable. This is because the so-called academic courses of education have tended to neglect practical aspects, and vocational courses have been so designed that they are perceived as courses meant for less bright students. It would be advisable to devise certain such vocational courses which would demand a very high degree of brightness from students and teachers, and some vocational courses should be developed right upto the levels of post graduation and research.

Holistic Vision

At present, syllabus for each subject is drawn up almost in isolation from other subjects. This encourages learning by snippets. Hence, a holistic view of knowledge has to be kept in view in formulating curricula and syllabii.

Need to Update Curricula

On account of explosion of information, there is

continuous pressure to update the contents of various subjects of study. However, very little thought is being given to prune those contents which have become outdated or receded into the background. The load on children is being increased year after year because no effort has been initiated to revise and prune the curricula, and there is no agency in the country which is solely devoted to the task of formulating appropriate curricula keeping in view the advancement of knowledge, obsolescence of discarded theories and data, as also the holistic standpoint. There is a need to create a national body of the most eminent experts who could be given this task as a continuing and permanent occupation. This body could be subdivided into groups and sub-groups, but it should be able to provide a wide vision that can guide appropriate connections and inter-relationships between subjects and level of studies.

Value Education

A special care has to be taken, while framing the curriculum, to ensure that the theme of value education receives utmost importance.

Indian Culture

National education should be able to project a true and inspiring account and message of Indian culture. This is an extremely difficult task, and it is yet an extremely important task. Without this, we shall not be able to deal rightly with the powerful external influences which are invading our country and creating too much of mechanical imitation, too much of sense of subordination and even servitude. To reject unintelligently anything because it is alien is both irrational and injurious. Besides, it is impossible. We have to assimilate with right discrimination all that is good and beneficial for ourselves and for the world. But this means that India has to recover its own centre and find its own base, and do whatever it has to in its own strength and genius. This will involve a great and devoted labour, and ultimately the fruits of this labour have to be translated into concrete terms of the contents of curricula and into corresponding teaching learning materials.

The national agenda for education must place this task on the top of its priorities.

Need to make Studies Interesting and Understandable

There is a legitimate complaint that the books and learning materials which are prescribed for studies have been written in such an uninteresting manner that they rarely evoke enthusiastic response from the students. Again, students in our country belong to different backgrounds, and a large number of them belong to a group of first generation learners. A large number of teachers do not themselves adequately understand the books that they are supposed to teach. A serious inquiry into this problem will suggest a radical recommendation which will have far, reaching repercussions on the entire system of textbook production. All those who are capable of thinking and acting in this important area will have to be engaged in meeting this problem.

Linguistic Competence

One of the basic problems in our country is related to linguistic competence that we should prescribe at various levels of education. Again, the present language policy has been injurious to the study of classical languages, and it is becoming clearer that our cultural identity cannot be retained if we continue to neglect these languages. Our cultural ethos is deeply rooted in the ancient languages like Sanskrit and Tamil and in medieval classical languages like Persian and Arabic. Our curricula have to be so designed so that our students are at least able to appreciate the original resources of our culture.

While it is true that mother tongue should be a natural medium of instruction, the importance of international languages like English and French have to be recognized, —particularly, when forces of globalization are mounting day by day. A fresh study of the various problems relating to the linguistic competence in the entire educational system needs to be studied. Once again, this study will suggest radical recommendations, the implementation of which must occupy a high place among the priorities of the national agenda.

Methods of Education

Need for Innovative Methods

At first sight, it might seem that in a situation where even the primary articles and equipment like blackboards are not adequately provided in our primary schools, any discussion or recommendation in respect of methods of education and innovations in this area should be regarded as irrelevant or too premature. And yet, this subject is of great importance, and it must be taken in hand in right earnest.

As a matter of fact, the methodology of education has not received much attention since the time when the British system of education was introduced in our country except during the movement for national education and in the context of the great experiments which came to be initiated and developed under the inspiration of leaders like Maharishi Dayananda Saraswati, Swami Vivekananda, Dr. Rabindra Nath Tagore, Mahatma Gandhi and Sri Aurobindo. As a result, methods of lecturing and the use of blackboard have remained the only methods of education in our country. If the same old system and old methodologies are allowed to be continued, we shall be running the risk of keeping our children at a great disadvantage, which is bound to result in keeping our country perpetually poor economically, educationally and culturally.

Child-Centred Education

The national agenda for education must, therefore, advocate at least the following elements of what may be called innovative and dynamic methods of education.

a) The teaching-learning methods must look upon the child not as an inert material to be shaped by external pressing machines but as a living entity that is capable of creative participation through questioning, inquiring and through total involvement in the learning process.

b) The child should be treated with great sympathy and understanding, and methods of coercion have to be totally replaced by methods that give room to suggesting but not imposing, to freedom that does not amount to license, and to discipline that is not external but which grows into self-discipline.

c) A great emphasis should be laid on learning by doing and learning by practicing which would require different methods that are appropriate to cognition, affection and conation; and

d) A great emphasis should be laid on self-study, project work, group discussions, community work, activities of adventure and works of manual labour.

Need for New Learning Materials

New learning materials will also have to be prepared which should be appropriate to these dynamic methods of education.

Counselling Services

The world in which we are living today is getting

increasingly impersonalized, mechanized, and those who are in need of guidance find blank and impersonal walls around them creating disappointment and cynisim. There is, therefore, a great need to create agencies in educational institutions and also elsewhere which can provide mature and wise counsel to all those who are in need of it.

Students, in particular, need to have wide ranging and unbiased advice in respect of their studies, personal problems of friendships and relationships, development of their faculties, availability of opportunities, and various choices open to them for suitable vocations, professions and careers.

Parents are also in need of guidance, since they confront various problems as to how to deal with their children, their courses of studies, their problems connected with freedom, discipline, adolescence and growing youthfulness. They also need to help their children in respect of their homework and co-curricular activities. Every parent today is required to become a teacher and has to learn, if not formal methods of teaching, at least those informal methods which are directly relevant to home situations and to character development.

These problems need to be highlighted prominently in our society so that prior counselling services are made available to students and parents.

Problems of Drug Addiction and Aids

A most disconcerting phenomenon which is vastly spreading in our country is the use of drugs among teenagers and youths. Even the scourage of AIDS is spreading in our country.

These problems are extremely difficult, and it is unfortunate that they receive very little attention. It is therefore, necessary to study these problems in depth and propose and implement right measures to meet these problems.

Examination System

What Needs to be Changed?

The present system of examination, as operating in India, has come under severe criticism. And yet, nothing significant has been done to change this system. It has sometimes been suggested that examinations should altogether be abolished. This suggestion has been implemented in some parts of the country as far as primary education is concerned. Experience has shown that examinations or tests are in themselves necessary. What is required is the change in the nature of the tests, frequency of the tests, situations of the tests, purposes of the tests and the attitudes which have to be developed among students and teachers in regard to tests.

Right use of Tests

Tests can be used mainly for:

a) stimulation;

b) providing opportunities to the students to think clearly and to formulate ideas adequately;

c) achieving precision, exactness and mastery of details;

d) arriving at a global view of the subjects of works in question;

e) self-evaluation; and

f) gaining self-confidence.

If tests are woven into the learning process, the nature and frequency of the tests depend upon the above mentioned purposes which are to be fulfilled through the learning process.

Test for Character Development

It has often been argued that no system of tests can be

devised to evaluate students in respect of essential qualities which education for character development aims at, such as, those of truthfulness, sincerity, cheerfulness, benevolence, right judgment, courage, self-sacrifice, cooperation and harmony. This argument assumes that the system of tests that is prevalent today cannot be caged or only marginally changed. But, if students are required to maintain their progress reports on those activities, compositions, essays, artistic creations which they have participated in or produced and which in their own judgement are of a high quality, and if these progress reports of the minimum duration of three years, are subjected to scrutiny by a board of examination and further tested through an oral test, it would not be impossible to assess students' performance in respect of character development. Similarly if every student is required to pass a national physical test, a further avenue of assessments will be available. For maintenance of physical fitness will require regularity and punctuality in respect of participation in activities of physical education. Besides, a process of physical education will largely contribute to the development of some of the valuable qualities of team spirit, discpline, obedience and sportsmanship.

Tests and Teachers

Teachers will have to play a major role, if new systems of testing are to succeed. Teachers have to accept that testing is a necessary part of their duties, and they have to develop the requisite qualities which are required not only for the cross-examination of written papers but also those qualities which are to be promoted through various oral and practical tests.

Entrance Tests

One of the evils in our country that has recently become very prevalent is that of entrance tests which are being conducted by a number of institutions where students are required to appear— sometimes in a rapid succession within a short time or even on the same day. This is because major examinations of the country have come into disrepute and it has been widely recognised that they do not really examine the students properly. Employers, too, complain in the same way. There has also been a suggestion that jobs should be dissociated from degrees.

National Testing Service

In order to create a new situation so as to meet these difficulties, it may be suggested that tests for admission and for placement in the employment market should be conducted by a 'National Testing Service' and they should be open to anyone who wants to take them, irrespective of whether they hold any degree or certificate or not. These tests should be related to specific jobs for employment opportunities or certain specific pursuits of studies and disciplines of knowledge and skills. These tests should be three-fold written tests, oral tests and practical tests. These tests should further be reinforced by the above-mentioned methods of scrutinising progress reports of the candidates as also by the physical fitness tests.

Higher Education and Research

Neglect of higher education under the fragile suggestion that the state must devote all its major attention and resources largely to elementary education is perilous. Education cannot be divided into compartments, and hence, higher education will have to be regarded as important as primary and secondary education. Without higher education, and that too, of a very high quality, we shall suffer from unemployable graduates, incompetent teachers and second rate or third rate professionals. Again, the entire world is global, and we have to ensure that the global frontiers of knowledge and research can be nourished in our institutions of higher education.

There is no denying the fact that meaningful higher education is very expensive. The government, therefore, should provide as much as it possibly can towards higher education.

At the same time, higher educational institutions should be promoted and encouraged to come up in the private sector. It should be made mandatory that no one charges more than 20% of the recurring expenditure as tuition fee and that no student admitted is allowed to drop because of financial reasons.

Reforms suggested for national changes among teachers, students, parents and national administrators will apply equally to all sectors of education, including higher education. Reforms in regard to contents and methods of education as also in regard to examination system have to be carried out with the help of the best teachers and educationists, even those who have retired from active service, should be provided with facilities and opportunities, particularly in the People's Council of Education, so that they are able to contribute the ripe fruits of their long experience, professional competence and wisdom.

The problem of accountability is extremely important. And we have to emphasize the accountability has to come from the top. Several examples can be cited to show how people, when they demonstrate accountability and personal integrity, various problems discipline, finances and relationships have been resolved with great efficiency and thoroughness.

Areas of research have to be widely and wisely enlarged. Inter-disciplinarity and holistic research are increasingly gaining relevance. It is at the higher levels of research that major themes such as the synthesis of the knowledge of Matter with the knowledge of the Spirit can be rightly dealt with so as to meet the growing aspiration in humanity to realise inter dependence between science and values, and even between science and spirituality.

Conclusion

Let us not forget the essentials. Gurudev Rabindra Nath Tagore has written a short story "*The Parrot's* Training", the moral of which is that whatever structures we may build for education, whatever facilties and opportunities we may create for students and teachers, nothing will be of any real use if we forget that education should subserve the highest interests of the child who is a living entity. And if we place the child in a system that would imprison its free and living movements and if we stuff the child with plethora of materials, the child will get suffocated and may even wither away.

Let us, therefore, create for our children and youth, nurseries of living souls where they can blossom like smiling and shining flowers, spreading their fragrance by their vibrating freshness and youthfulness.

This shall be the soul of the national agenda for education.

Chapter-II
Global Perspective of Value Based Education

Introduction

The *Bhagvad Gita* says, "There is nothing in the world so sacred as knowledge. He who is perfected by yoga, all round development finds in the fullness of time".

According to Ramamurti Committee Report(1990) "Education must further provide a climate for the nurture of values, both as a personalized set of values, forming one's character and including necessarily social, cultural and national values, so as to have a context and meaning for actions and decisions, and in order to enable the persons to act with conviction and commitment,"

The UNESCO Reports (2000: 93.) said, "Education shall be directed to the full development of the human personality and to the strengthening of respect for human rights and fundamental freedoms. It shall promote understanding, tolerance and friendship among all nations, racial and religious groups, and shall further the activities of the United Nations for the maintenance of Peace.

In simple terms, civilization and culture deal with provision and vision. Civilization arranges provision and caters to provisionary aspects, and culture provides vision of how to use the provision. The 'how' of the last sentence leads to questions of values, morals and ethics? All three as different domains share the common premise of 'worthy' and 'standard' manners and conduct of men. Since they can be acquired, so they fall under the category of education as the means of imparting these values, morals and ethical standards. In the given spectrum, education is not only the manifestation of infinite already inherent in a human being but also means of transferring the acquired knowledge from one generation to the next. Hence, in a world mired in anarchy of valuelessness, there is stress on the role of value education and also on the role of institutions of higher education as the facilitators of values. The UNESCO report mentions:

"The contemporary world is too often a world of violence that believes the hope some people placed in human progress... Is it possible to devise a form of education which might make it possible to avoid conflicts or resolve them peacefully by developing respect for other people, their culture and their spiritual values? The idea of teaching non violence in schools is laudable even if it is only one means among many for combating the prejudices that lead to conflict."

According to Prof. A. K. Singh the stress on the value education is indicative of crisis of values, and that the present education system has failed in facilitating the process. The education system is information-based. The fact, however is that information should move knowledge, and knowledge towards wisdom. In a state of absence of wisdom the society would head for anarchy of valuelessness. Without wisdom the society and the bearers of information would not know what to do with it or how to use it properly. D.S. Kothari observed in this regard:

The fundamental values of life, integrity, pursuit of truth and idealism cannot be sustained by embalming these in monuments and memorials or by inscribing them in textbooks. High ideals and great national goals are meaningless, unless we strive for them passionately and ceaselessly. And each generation has to recreate, revitalize and renovate these through hard work and sacrifice, otherwise ideals and values wither and decay and goals fade away. (Kothari 2000:447) He further remarked:

"For man's material, cultural and spiritual wellbeing and these are inextricably interdependent we need both Ahimsa and Science. All men are equal, are brothers, is a supreme moral truth. It is reinforced by modern Science. So in theory the ethic of equality, but in practice it would remain no more than a pious dream, totally beyond man's reach unless both Ahimsa and Science find equally a place in our lives: without Ahimsa and Science man has no future." (Kothari 2000: 459)

All religions and major thinkers of the world have stressed the need for value orientation of the society.

Worldwide Programme of Education[1]

The astounding communications technology, which today encircles the globe seldom uses its tremendous potential to spread global values and foster a more caring, compassionate consiousness. On the contrary, the media is full of violence and horror, cruelty and carnage, unbridled consumerism and unabashed promiscuity, which not only distorts the awareness of the young but dulls our sensitivity to the problems of human suffering and pain. What is urgently needed, therefore, is a U-turn in our educational and communication policies. We need to develop carefully structured programms on a global scale based clearly and unequivocally on the premises that human survival involves the growth of a creative and compassionate global consciousness. The spiritual dimension will have to be once

1. *Collected speech of Honurable Karan Singh Ji (M.P.) delivered in India International Center*

again given importance in our thinking, and for this we must draw upon the great reservoir of idealism and spiritual values provided by the rich and varied religious traditions of humanity.

We need the courage to think globally, to break away from traditional paradigms and plunge boldly into the future. We must so mobilize our inner and outer resources that we begin consciously to build a new world in the twenty-first century based on mutually assured welfare rather than mutually assured destruction. As global citizen committed to human survival and welfare, we must structure a worldwide programme of education—for children and adults alike—that would open their eyes to the realities of the new global age that is dawning and open their hearts to the anguished cry of the disadvantaged and the deprived. And there is no time to be lost. With the emergence of the global society, the sinister forces of fundamentalism and fanaticism, of exploitation and intimidation, are also gathering strength.

In the restructuring of the entire educational process for the twenty-first century, two more factors are critical. The first is the prime importance of human resources in the process of renovation. The report of the UNESCO International Commission on Education for the Twenty-first Century has stressed that the role of the teacher will remain critical despite the emerging technological innovations. Indeed, the very existence of this new pedagogic paradigm will involve a higher level of expertise and a constant enhancing of skills if teachers are to cope with the new challenges. The old concept of rigid curricula and routine teaching is no longer valid. In the new dispensation, the teacher will have to be intellectually motivated and academically challenged on an on-going basis. In my view it should be mandatory for all teachers to upgrade their skills on a continuing basis at least once every five years, and this will involve significant administrative and managerial devices. Even if today's teacher cannot live up to the ancient Indian concept of the *Guru* (one who dispels the darkness), he or she must continue to fulfil the leadership requirements and become a role model for the students.

The second aspect relates to community and family involvement in educational management. Here again, the UNESCO International Commission, chaired by Jacques Delors, has unequivocally stated that education cannot be looked at in isolation from the social and familial environment of the child. Indeed the first school for child is the family, and the first teacher, the parents. The unfortunate compartmentalization between the family and the school on the one hand, and the school and the community on the other, is now widely prevalent. This dichotomy needs to be resolved, and the educational process once again re-fashioned as a joint endeavour of family and community with a creative symbiosis of both. There are several modalities for achieving it, including parent-teacher associations, community involvement and civic participation. As we move into the twenty-first century, with the whirlwind of changes sweeping across the world, it is necessary to further strengthen these interlinkages so that the community becomes the sheet including the rights of the child, especially of the girl child.

While a whole range of human activity provides the subject matter of Fundamental Education, each particular programme should give first attention to the most pressing needs and problems of the community concerned. The content, therefore, varies widely with circumstances, but on the long run it should include the development of qualities to fit man to live in the modern world, such as personal

2. *NCERT 2000:34-35*

judgement and initiative, freedom from fear and superstition sympathy and understanding for different points of view. Spiritual and moral development; belief in ethical ideals, and the habit of acting upon them with the duty to examine traditional standards of behaviour; and to modify them to suit new conditions.

The Delor's Commission, UNESCO, 1996 made recommendations regarding the steps to be taken for implementing global values in a culturally pluralistic world.

"Education in tolerance and respect for other people, a prerequisite for democracy, should be regarded as a general and ongoing enterprise. Values in general and tolerance in particular cannot be taught in the strict sense; the desire to impose from the outside predetermined values comes down on the end to negotiating them, since values only have meaning when they are freely chosen by the individual. At the very most, therefore, schools may facilitate the daily practice of tolerance by helping pupils to allow for the points of view of others and by encouraging the discussion of moral dilemmas or cases involving ethical crises.

It should, however, be the school's role to explain to young people the historical, cultural or religious background to the various ideologies, competing for their attention in the society around them or in the school and classroom. This task of explanation which could possibly be carried out with the help of outsiders is a delicate one, since it must avoid giving offence and can bring politics and religion, generally banned from the classroom, into school. Adolescents can thus be helped to build their system of thought and values freely and in full knowledge of facts, without succumbing blindly to the dominant influences, thus acquiring greater maturity and open mindedness. One can in this way, lay

3. UNESCO 2000: 27

the foundations of future harmony and peace by encouraging democratic dialogue."

Some of the values are culture-specific, and others eternal. In the global world, the global values like democracy have come into existence. The Ramamurti Committee enumerated some of these values in the following manner:

"Democracy, secularism, socialism, scientific temper, equality of sexes, honesty, integrity, courage and justice (fairness), respect for all life forms, different cultures and languages (including tribal) etc. constitute the mosaic of values which is vital to the unity and integrity of the country. The content and process of education should be all pervasively informed by these basic values." [4]

The Four Pillars of Education [5]

The Delors Report probes deeply into the challenges of inculcating traditional and moral values in the educational management. It has identified four pillars of education—

1. Learning to know
2. Learning to do
3. Learning to be
4. Learning to live together

By addressing all these four dimensions effectively we can hope to structure a better society for humanity in the twenty-first century. Learning to know involves intellectual ability which will have to function on a continuing basis in this changing world of science and technology.

Learning to do is associated with the acquisition of skills, including manual skills, that enables a person to become a creative and useful member of society. Learning to be is the deepest concept. It implies a movement inwards, towards

4. *Rama Murti Committee 1990, MHRD Govt of India*
5. *Delors Report international commission on education*

the depth of our psyche to find the light and the strength to behave as responsible and creative citizens in the emerging global society. And finally, learning to live together is the very basis upon which this society has to be founded. Fanaticism, fundamentalism, exclusivism, hostility, enmity and feuding have no place in a society which is bound together now by instant communications, satellite technology and con-ceptual convergence. Taken together, these four pillars represent the great challenge that all of us who claim to be educationists must boldly face.

What we need, then, is a holistic philosophy based upon the following premises:

a) That the planet we inhabit and of which we are all citizens—planet earth is a single, living, pulsating entity; that the human race in the final analysis is an interlocking, extended family—*Vasudhaiva Kutumbakam* as the *Veda* has it; and that differences of race and religion, nationality and ideology, sex and sexual preference, economic and social are viewed in the broader context of global unity;

b) That the ecology of planet earth has to be preserved from mindless destruction and ruthless exploitation, and enriched for the welfare of generations yet unborn; and that there should be a more equitable consumption pattern based on limits to growth, not unbridled consumerism;

c) That hatred and bigotry, fundamentalism and fanaticism, greed and jealousy, whether among individuals, groups or nations are corrosive emotions which must be overcome as we move into the next century; and that love and compassion, caring and charity, friendship and cooperation are the elements that have to be encouraged as we transit into a new global awareness;

d) That the world's great religions must no longer fight against each other for supremacy, but mutually cooperate for the welfare of the human race; and, through a creative and continuing inter-faith dialogue (instead of the dogma and exclusivism that divides them,) the golden thread of spiritual aspiration that binds them together must be nurtured:

e) That the new, holistic education must acknowledge the multiple dimensions of human personality— physical, intellectual, aesthetic, emotional and spiritual—and seek a harmonious development of an integrated human being, and a massive and concerted drive is needed to eradicate the scourge of illiteracy worldwide by the year 2010, with special emphasis on female literacy, particularly in the developing countries.

Global Initiative for Value Based Education

Day after day, the media brings more and more stories of violence and terrorism, acts of injustice and exploitation from many parts of the world and from our country as well. Discoveries and developments in areas of science and technology have more often been used for exploitative and destructive purposes. The world spends about one billion US dollars every year for producing and operationalizing weapons of mutual destruction, while one adult in three cannot read or write, and one person in four goes to bed hungry in our country. This is true in several other developing countries as well.

It is no wonder (but nevertheless it comes as a surprise) that the United Nations convened the Millennium World Peace Summit of religious and spiritual leaders at the United Nations from 28 to 31 August 2000. Citing a reason for this initiative, UN said that despite the best efforts of individual religious and spiritual leaders from different parts of the world, the human family is still unable to prevent the eruption of horrible acts of war. During the last decade, more than hundred armed conflicts have erupted in over seventy different locations around the world. Since the end of the Second World War, 27 million people have lost their lives due to war. Although religious leaders individually have spoken out against and tried to halt these hostilities, until now, there has been no concerted effort to join the world's leading religious figures in a united initiative for world peace, working in conjunction with the United Nations. Even today, 83 per cent of the world's population adheres to a formal religious or spiritual belief system. Today, religious differences continue to be a cause of conflicts in many parts of the world, despite the fact that the religious leaders call upon their followers to adopt a new vision of tolerance and cooperation. Today there are many examples of religious communities cooperating to resolve conflict and rebuild society. The delegates of this historic World Peace Summit took a number of concrete steps to declare their commitment to work more closely as a community of spiritual leaders and with the community of the United Nations. They worked together to discern shared commitment to peace expressed in a Declaration for World Peace. Moreover, an International Advisory Council of Religious and Spiritual Leaders was formed to work with the United Nations in peace-making and peace-keeping efforts. This Council added a unique spiritual dimension to the United Nations difficult task of mediating conflicts between nations and among peoples from different religious and ethnic groups. In the frame of reference of our Constitution, by giving substance to the ideal and the goal that it sets before every citizen, offering freedom, equality, justice and unity or fraternity to all and thus bring about a new Indian renaissance.

The Present Scenario in India

Many in our country are happy at the great progress

and the accumulation of wealth that India has achieved, over the past decade. But since this situation only relates to minority of the people while the majority still waits to have the basics of human life. There are doubts as to whether this prosperity is sustainable. It is estimated that in India today 380 million people do not have a square meal a day. There is an urgent call from many quarters for a more equitable and just society, where the fruit of our economy are shared in fair measure. This was the point that Nobel Laureate Dr Amratya Sen made.

According to Father Kunnukal the brilliant performance of India as an emerging world economic power provides a palliative and even an incentive for unscrupulous behaviour. In the mad rush for money, power and for getting ahead, the individual has often been pushed aside and relationships are sacrificed. Yet, we see a hopeful sign. International big business is moving more and more into value-based and principle-centred actions and behaviour patterns, into placing greater stress on persons, rather than merely on things and products alone. The UNESCO Report put the focus on the inner dimension. It is interesting to note this shift from the outer to the inner dimension, in the context of an almost total emphasis in the world today on what can be seen, touched and measured in terms of the economic and the power dimensions alone. Principles are commonly and widely accepted norms and values which are based on a vision, a focus, a thrust area and normative guidelines for life and patterns of behaviour. So much stress is put on narrow individualistic concerns and conveniences that the rest of the people, even those immediately close to us are ignored. Our stress is on our rights, our needs, our comfort, whether these infringe on others' rights or not. Social discipline, social character is what we need in India to find acceptability by the world community and earn respect.

Otherwise the image of the *ugly Indian* will remain and will land us in increasing difficulties. And the flight from India will continue, as many Indians settle outside, where they know people conform to norms and standards while providing large amount of individual and group freedom to function effectively. They are not going out just for money.

Father Kunnukal further remarked: "This new India will not materialize if based merely on an economic or political agenda, since the real crisis facing India today is moral and spiritual. So this is where we can make a real contribution to the rebuilding of India. The President, in his Independence Day message, made several concrete directional statements, all very topical and contextual. In response to the signs of the times, I believe that the national effort and educational effort, within it, should be in the area of personal and institutional or societal empowerment through character and value education, namely to facilitate or animate people to live a principle based life, to care for others, to build a community of the Indian nation. Or to make a solid contribution to build up the weak social dimension of our national cultural ethos. Or to introduce the social dimension of character and social discipline into our lives. There is growing concern about the state of lawlessness in our country, not only by the dacoits and criminals, but also by the law-makers and even by the young sons and daughters of the affluent. It is therefore not surprising that the Government of India and the Ministry of HRD are keen to promote value education in schools. One avenue that has been chosen is through the inculcation of the Fundamental Duties, contained in Article 51 A of the Constitution. They contain exemplary goals as:

Promoting harmony and the spirit of common brotherhood transcending religious, linguistic and regional or sectional diversities;

- to renounce practices derogatory to the dignity of women;
- to value and preserve the rich heritage of our composite culture;
- to protect and improve the national environment;
- to develope scientific temper;
- to abjure violence;
- to strike towards excellence in all spheres of individual and collective quality so that the nation instantly rises to high levels of endeavour and achievement.

Conflict between Globalization and Value-Orientation

One of the most serious problems that is being faced by our society today is the rapid degradation of our cultural heritage which is the mirror of our values, morals, customs etc. The present condition of our society is changing rapidly with new innovations of technologies and modern means of communication. Every individual is in cut throat competition of material achievement and has transformed the human being to a mechanical robot. 'Status', and 'Good salary package' are the two factors on which the rate of success of an individual is assessed. But, if this is so why is it that after achieving these goals also people are still 'frustrated' and 'unhappy'? Why are people with high status and position in the society hunting for mental peace? The answers to these questions may emerge from our inner soul itself. Today there is a total crisis of values. It is really surprising that country which was acknowledged by the world as the custodian of moral and spiritual ethics, where the King Harishchandra sacrificed his wife and son for truth is today facing problems like terrorism, embezzlement of public funds, molestation, robbery, corruption etc. It is easy to blame all these ills on our growing population but is that not a means to console ourselves? In India there has been a rapid erosion of social, moral, cultural, and political values. In the race of competition people have forgotten about their rich socio-cultural heritage. They have become indifferent towards their families. Joint families have segregated and most of the population has started confining themselves in to their narrow territory, and if required are ready to win the race at the cost of their motherland. People have become reluctant to their prior duties towards their families. In recent studies it has been found that most of the people are well acquainted about their Fundamental rights keeping aside the duties. Rights and duties are two sides of a same coin. It is quite obvious that one cannot be achieved without achieving the other.

Misconceptual notion of modernity, rapid growth of science and technology and the subsequent industrialization have caused a great threat and danger to our old morals and values. In the changed social set-up, our definitions of good morals, stand questioned. Old values seems to be lost and new are yet to be evolved and brought into practice.The present era can be termed as a 'transtional one'. Will Durent has very aptly put forth this phenomena. According to him, "These are the varied causes of our moral change. It is in terms of their transit from farms and houses to factories and city streets, that we must understand the generation which so boisteriously replaces us. Their lives and problems are new and different. The Industrial Revolution has them in its grip and transforms their customs, their garb, their work, their religion, and their conduct: to judge them in terms of the old code is as unfair and unhistorical as to force upon them the corsets and bustles, the beards and boots of our ancient days."

Several scientific inventions also have a role in

challenging our old and traditional, but very useful values to a great extent. It is difficult to compile a list of changes brought about by these scientific inventions in our daily life. Similarly it is not easy to compile a comprehensive list of 'good' or 'bad' actions of mankind—as moment after moment man is confronted with new situations and problems. It is said that the action, speech or thoughts which are motivated by or admixed with perverted emotions, called sex, lust, anger, greed, attachment, arrogance and sloth or lethargy (*kama, krodha, lobha, moha, mada* and *matsar*), called six sins, enemies of a man (*shadripu*).

Of these, sex-lust is the arch enemy of man; it is the chief sin or vice because due to this very weakness a man falls prey to other vices easily. But here also our scientific invention has come to 'rescue'. Contraceptives have intruded to adulterate the sanctity of individual's private life also. The invention and spread of contraceptives is the proximate cause of our changing morals. The old moral code restricted sexual experience to marriage, because copulation could not be effectively separated from parentage, but today the dissociation of sex from reproduction has created a situation unforseen by earliers generations. All the relations of man and woman are being changed by this one factor alone; and the moral code of the future will have to take account of these new facilities which invention has created.

Now-a-days newspapers, magazines and other news media are flooded with reports of crime, murder, agitation and eve-teasing. We read in newspapers of several such occurrences where landlords and tenants have bitter exchange and atercation leading to stabbing. Disputes between father and son, between wife and husband, between son-in-law and father-in-law are not rare. For want of endurance in one's dealings all family ties are broken, people leave homes forever out of disgust and anger. All these occurrences indicate deterioration in our ethical standards, loss of our moral and social values accruing great loss to families, society and the nation at large.

It is widely believed that modernization is responsible for the crisis in values to a large extent. The reasons are not far to seek. Modernization involves industrialization, use of modern and advanced techniques in agriculture and all other spheres of life and work. Within modernization comes better communication that bridge the gap not only between places but also between people. The result is that the traditional values of a small closely knit society which demands cooperation, loyalty, dependence on relations, neighbours get eroded and people tend to ignore these values. They become more self-reliant and self-centred which makes men more impersonal in their conduct. Had modern society consciously tried to retain or imbibe the values of self-discipline in individuals, the crisis of values that is so widespread could have been contained. Self-discipline teaches one not only to value ones rights but to respect those of others equally.

Incidents of violence and destruction are increasingly reported. People take irrational pleasure in discriminating between their faith and that of others and resort to communal riots. Strikes and lock-outs are becoming more and more common-place. Rarely does one read the newspaper without coming across an item reporting strikes, lock-outs and crime. Few people realise that strikes and lock-outs hamper the economic development and advancement of society. The total loss which the people suffer due to such antisocial and antinational movements runs into millions of rupees each year. The major cause of such incidents is the loss of self-discipline in the average human-being, who is taken in by anitnationalistic elements and ignores his duty therby harming the economy and thus society in general.

Lack of self-discipline has led to an ignorance of one's

values and duty which has adversely affected the structure of the society in the modern day. Indian society has also been affected by this trend and the process of disintegration of our basic social infrastructure and system is discernible all around. The hazards we now face are far more dimensional than we had ever imagined earlier. Nietzsche says "When a tree grows up to heaven, its roots reach down to hell." We must not therefore be overwhelmed by the failure of many individuals to maintain self-discipline. Instead, we must try to make them understand, as Dr. Radhakrishnan wrote "Error is not crime, it is only youth, immaturity, which can be controlled and corrected with the right effort."

This process of disintegration of values would soon prove to be disastrous. Unless a conscious effort is made to reverse this trend and to inculcate in one and all, a spirit of discipline of the self. This cannot be done by simple physical processes. The initiation of the spirit and the awakening of the mind are the two modes of efficiently implanting values such as discipline of the self in people in all walks of life. Whittier has written "When faith is lost, when honour dies, the man is dead."

Thus any man can be called a man as long as he guards his values, as soon as they are gone, the very reason for his being called 'human' vanishes and he is lowered to the level of animals. Let every man realise that his values are guarded by his conscience and that these are not derived by nature or from reason, but by custom.

The crying need of the modern society is to inculcate the spirit of self-discipline and the values that follows from it, in every individual, from his childhood, through proper education and training.

Without any values, the world could not be a place worth living in and, unfortunately, it is heading towards this state due to the present crisis. If no person is interested in life, in the true sense of the word, then we can carry on without bothering at present. But it is obviously not so. The trend towards modernity is being grossly misinterpreted to mean removal of values. We witness very often a total lack of regard for the values of others amongst people. Today, very few people care for or have respect for age old values— like freedom, belief, sincerity and self-respect, the right to work and freely express one's views. While we cherish individually these values for ourselves, we show a total disregard for similar values of others. Very rarely are people found making true sacrifices for the benefit of others, selfishness fills the atmosphere and corruption and other immoral acts reflect totally corrupted values. Individuals take pleasure in misleading strangers. Most people today refrain from or at least avoid taking so-called "unnecessary' responsibilities making themselves morally accountable for some particular things, whether done by one or the other. Very few people are disciplined enough to fulfil and do justice to such responsibilities and duties, though they heartfully partake of all benefits they can derive from taking that responsibility.

India used to take pride in its rich traditions, art, culture, ideals and teachings of great personalities. But all these seem to be dormant and polluted to large extent. Our media has failed in providing desired nourishment to our culture. On the contrary, due to commercial type of competition in gaining cheap popularity and material benefits, they (media) have polluted our culture. Because of this cultural pollution, our work-culture has also been polluted. It is this polluted work-culture that has affected the sincerity and devotion to duty in various walks of life. That is why we come across the incidents referred to above. Self-discipline and self-restraint are the need of the hour in today's Society. Discipline is regarded as a check on one's liberty or ceiling on one's right. In these circumstances, it is vital that inner discipline is generated among the new generation. It should not be a sort of imposition, but should be more and more practical. In education, therefore, we need a genuine faith in the existence of moral principles which are capable of effective application. This application requires to be in the social-settings. John Dewey, a noted educationist, has rightly remarked on this point. According to him, "To isolate the formal relationship of citizenship from the whole system of relations with which it is actually interwoven; to suppose that there is someone particular study or mode of treatment which can make the child a good citizen; to suppose, in other words, that a good citizen is anything more than a thoroughly efficient and serviceable member of society, one with all his powers of body and mind under control, is a hampering superstition which it is hoped may soon disappear from educational discussion.

"Therefore, in moral education indoctrination should be avoided and defects of value clarification and cognitive developmentalism should be removed by the educators, before they plan any strategy of value-oriented education. It will be possible when the teacher avoids imposing his own judgements or ideals and approving or disapproving the moral judgement of the individuals under his or her charge."

In America (U.S.A) " In the past decade the topic of moral education in the schools has received a great deal of discussion. In part this is a response to a variety of events that have, to say the least, shaken public life; Vietnam. Watergate, Koreagate as well as tales of perfidy and corruption in industry, unions, and in the professions. As usual, the schools have received their bit of the blame for allowing us to come to this sorry state through the indictment that they are failing to morally educate individuals. And since the schools, contrary to many observations, are one of the least rigid institutions in our society, educators have scrambled to include some component on moral education in the curriculum". Similarly in our country also many schools specially convent schools have some sort of moral education in their curriculum. Certain periods are allotted to moral education.

But our experiences have revealed that moralizing has not served the purpose in the past nor is it serving the purpose in the present. It becomes a mechanical process, neither does it touch the heart nor provide any scope for intellectual exercise. On the contrary, it becomes problematic specially when the question of indoctrination is raised. As values are governed by metaethical relativism, moralizing appears to be a form of indoctrination. Therefore, the strategy of value-oriented education is a challenge for teachers, parents and the society at large.

In this context the observations made by Dr. Mary B. Lane Quentin baker in the book, *Our schools: Frontline for the 21st century* are very relevant.

"Concern for all human beings is humanism's ethical ideal. It underscores the worth and dignity of the individual and the welfare of humanity. Humanism elevates man. It presupposes an awareness of the need for the qualities associated with creativity, i.e. intuitiveness, empathy, passion and compassion. Caring is a key word in humanistic values. To be human means to feel and think beyond the present moment. We can do this because we have words—language which gives us a past and a future. To care is to see people as individuals, not as members of a class or a group. To care is to listen not as a routine but placing himself in another person's place. We live in a culture that is permeated by alienation and violence. Hence the need for incorporating humanistic values in our educational system. In order to transform the educational process into one anchored in human values, three attitudinal changes are needed. These are:

i) Trusting relationship,

ii) Eliminating hierarchies of worth, and

iii) Accepting that the learning ability of each human is infinite.

Introduction of cross-cultural education has been advocated, designed to uplift children to give them imagination and help them experience diversity. They have also pleaded development of self-awareness in our children so that they know the ground they stand on while maintaining a sense of wonder.

Cross-Cultural Education

According to Prof. Dhar a well known educationist cross-cultural education creates the problem of balancing between a sense of cultural enrichment and a sense of threat of getting subsumed. The values of society at large affect the children's perception of themselves and their cultural heritage, encouraging acceptance or antipathy towards the values of their own and other cultural groups within the society. This is so because of the factors that go to determine our ethnicity. These are self-identity, ascribed identity, cultural identity, racial identity, nationality and our descent. Prof. Daphne M. Keats, formerly of the University of New Castle, Australia has analysed this point in his book, *Culture and the Child.* He says:

"Goals of development are influenced by culture, parental status, religious affiliation, political environment, etc. the goals of development may include skill in inter-personal relationship, knowledge and competence. Culture plays a significant role in achieving these goals. There are many ways to ensure these: encouragement of punishment or some degree of modeling of the desired behaviour. The young child neither knows what the values of the culture are nor behaves according to a set of values. Rather, coming to know, accept and internalize the values of one's culture is a gradual developmental process. This process begins with the child responding to simple prescriptions and proscriptions, then generalising to other similar situations, and finally recognizing that these are abiding ways to think, feel and behave as a member of one's own culture. Many young adolescents, confused and lacking in the certainty of their own values, rebel, run away, get into bad company and argue with elders who appear to thwart their immediate desires. To escape their dilemmas, playing loud pop music, video games, just hanging around with other teenagers and experimenting with drugs and alcohol offer some temporary refuge."

Role of the Society and the Family in Global Perspective

Having thus established a need for incorporating values in the educational system, we must keep in mind that the real teaching comes from the family, the society and the school. In our younger days a religious teacher used to take all the children of our area to the riverbank. There he would explain the basics of physical cleaning accompanied, of course, by specified mantras. Thereafter he would take a class of all of us in a room adjacent to the temple. What he taught us there, I came to know in my later years, was the crux of the *Taittriya Upanishad.* There is hardly any household where the parents do not teach these lessons, knowingly or unknowingly, to their children. These were the same lessons, which are traditionally given to the students of Sanskrit, at the time of Deekshanta-modern day convocation: '*Satyam vada*—speak the truth': '*Dharmam chara*—do your assigned duty'; *Swadhyat ma pramadah*—shirk not from self-study'; *Pitri devo bhava*— treat your father with reverence (oliterally. as god) *Matri devo bhava*— treat your mother with reverence'; *Acharya devo bhava*— treat your teacher with reverence'; *Atithi devo bhava*- treat your guest with respect'. Then he would narrate to us stories, from the *Upanishads*, *puranas* and the two epics, the *Ramayana* and the *Mahabharata* as also *Panchatantra* and other collections from the Sanskrit literature. These stories brought home to us the importance of truth, sincerity, piety, brotherhood, compassion, honesty and other moral and ethical values. Ours was a joint family. This by itself taught us love and affection, duties and responsibilities, obedience and discipline. In addition, good behaviour and respect towards elders in the neighbourhood, friends circle and relations of the family were also taught, both by precept and by example. In schools also our classmates came from different religious groups, different classes of the society and even from different linguistic groups. Our teachers also were from different backgrounds. This environment inculcated in us a sense of fellow feeling and brotherhood, in the wider sense of the term. It may be concluded that despite the external influences of schooling, society and modern areas of exposure like the media, television, the family remains the primary source of value transmission. This does not, however, minimize the importance of the schools as a powerful supplementary source. In a collectivist society such as India, the individual is not the main focus. The socially effective person is one who is a good group member, who honours mutual obligations and develops the social skills necessary for creating harmonious relationship with others. It is also to be noted that in places like ours, where people are from different cultures or form a composite culture, tolerance is often the only practical course to maintain a peaceful life. Understanding acceptance and mutual respect must accompany tolerance. This does not mean that one party simply ignores the other. For in that case the relationship will be fragile and may change abruptly when one group of the composite society feels threatened by the other group, either physically, politically or culturally.

In order to avoid any such threat perception, it is necessary for us to incorporate the values of all the groups in our syllabus, curriculum, textbooks and training packages. These values, we shall soon find, may on the surface to be appear different but are basically the same in essence. The difference is because of the different setting, the different language and the different circumstances in which these have been formulated and prescribed.

Conclusion

From the above elaborate discussion it will be clear that Value Education is a much broader concept than Moral Education. Moral Education is a traditional term whereas Value Education is a new concept which has not even been well founded in our educational terminology, especially in the Indian perspective. In order to make Value Education more effective we should adopt a new approach to value education through different subjects. For this it is essential to understand properly the relationship of Moral Education to the broader concept of Value Education. Subsequently we should plan our strategies as per availability of time environment and other desired resources.

Inculcation or teaching of Value is a great task for teachers and other informal agencies including homes involved therein. For them the following recommendations put forth by International commission will be quite useful—

"The teacher's duty is less to inculcate and more and more to encourage thinking: his formal functions apart, he will have to become more and more an adviser, a partner to talk to; someone who helps seek out conflicting arguments rather than handing out ready-made truths. He will have to devote more time and energy to productive and creative activities: interaction, discussion, stimulation, understanding, encouragement".

The commission further points out that "One of the essential tasks of educators at present is to change the mentalities and qualifications inherent in all professions; thus they should be the first to be ready to rethink and change the criteria and basic situation of the teaching profession, in which the job of educating and stimulating students is steadily superseding that of simply giving instruction."

Chapter-III
Classification and Source of Values

Introduction

Keeping in view the nature of professional requirements values can be classified into several categories; such as—Economic Values, Social Values, Political Values, Spiritual Values, Modern Values, Aesthetic Values, Religious Values, Material Values etc. It is a matter of great regret that in our society value systems in the fields like politics, trade etc. are not encouraging and inspiring to the young generation.

There is wide discrepancy between what people do and what they say. Many political leaders, business executives, military leaders, workers of all sorts and even professional are known to do things that are inconsistent with what they say are their values. Charges of corruption are not unusual, and people can be bought. All this clearly suggests that approaches to values that have been so widely used in the past have been quite ineffective.

In the *'Documents on Social, Moral and Spiritual Values in Education'*, a booklet published by NCERT, a list of 83 values is appended. In this list there are values like abstinence, citizenship, cleanliness, compassion, courtesy, devotion, duty, endurance, fellow-feeling, honesty; gratitude, kindness, purity, regularity, self-help, self-control, team work etc. As stated earlier these terms are akin to the terms described as virtues in our scriptures.

Basic Values of all Religions

There are certain Values common to all religions like Hinduism, Sikhism, Jainism, Buddhism etc. Forty such values (virtues) are enumerated below with brief explanations:-

1. **Harmlessness—*(Ahimsa)***—implies refraining from injury to anyone through mind, speech or action.
2. **Truth (Satya)**—implies representing a thing precisely as one has perceived it through the mind or the senses, and in agreeable language.
3. **Non-stealing**—implies refraining from all forms of theft or illegal possession of other's property.
4. ***Brahmacharya* (Abstinence)**—consists of abstaining from all the eight forms of sexual gratification.
5. **Non-accumulation of things**—implies refraining from accumulation, from a sense of possession.
6. **Purity**—connotes freedom from bodily and mental impurities.
7. **Contentment**—refers to complete absence of thirst for material objects.
8. **Austerity**—implies enduring hardships for discharging one's religious obligations.
9. **Scriptural Study**—includes study of sacred books, repetition of Divine Names and recounting the virtues of the lord.
10. **Devotion to God**—is expressed through faith in and attachment to God.
11. **Spiritual Wisdom**—implies discrimination between real and unreal.

12. **Dispassion**—denotes complete absence of attachment to any thing pertaining to this world or the next.
13. **Self-discipline**—means exercising control over the mind.
14. **Control of the senses**—There are five senses of perception and five organs of action. Their control means bringing them all under subjugation and using them according to one's discretion.
15. **Endurance**—is the capacity to bear heat and cold and to remain unaffected by pleasure and pain etc. that is not to be influenced by diverse experiences.
16. **Piety**—means absolute faith in the *Vedas*, the scriptures and the teaching of Mahatmas. One's preceptor truths. It may also be termed as 'Purity'
17. **Forgiveness**—implies entertaining no thought of inflicting punishment on one who has wronged you.
18. **Courage**—refers to boldness i.e. absence of cowardice.
19. **Compassion (*Karma*)**—implies melting of the heart at the sight of suffering of a creature. It is termed as 'consideration' for others or 'fellow feeling' by the psychologists.
20. **Sublimity**—'Sublimation' is well-known term in 'psycho-analysis. In our scriptures it is equated with *'Tej'*. It is the power of superior souls under whose influence, even those who are attached to worldly enjoyments and are of a base nature, are deterred from sinful acts and take to noble pursuits including the excellence in fine arts etc.
21. **Arjava**—is the modern terminology which refers to 'simple living' which involves straightness of body, the senses and mind.
22. **Unselfishness**—means not seeking satisfaction of any selfish desire connected with this world or the next. In

the NCERT list of values it is termed as 'common cause' and 'common good'.

23. **Amanitva**—This consists in not seeking honour, respect or homage for oneself and observes ' gentlemanliness' or show 'respect for others'. These two values are included in the list given in NCERT booklet.
24. **Freedom from hypocrisy**—Hypocrisy consists in putting up a false show of 'piety' or purity'. This should be avoided scrupulously by all because one cannot fool all the persons at all the times.
25. **Absence of the back-biting spirit**—Back-biting or slandering proceeds generally from jealousy and this should be completely eschewed.
26. **Straight forwardness**—It means not attempting to achieve any thing from a selfish motive
27. **Humility**—This is the antonym of 'boasting' meaning to have very high estimate of oneself.
28. **Fortitude**—It means not to be perturbed in the face of the greatest difficulty and danger.
29. **Spirit of Service**—implies constantly striving to the best of one's ability through mind, speech and body and in a disinterested spirit to contribute to the happiness of all creatures according to their respective need. It indicates many values like concern for others, co-operation, compassion, fellow-feeling, helpfulness, humanism etc.
30. **Satsang (Good company)**—In its religious sense it means association with saints and holy men.
31. **Japa**—It is muttering or mental repetition of name of God or of a *Mantra* (sacred formula). It is different from meditation in some respects.

32. **Meditation**—It means concentration of the mind on a form of God to which one is specially attached.

33. **Freedom from malice**—It means entertaining no enmity even towards an enemy.

34. **Fearlessness (courage)**—refers to complete absence of fear.

35. **Evenmindedness (Equality) or Equanimity**—construced as looking on all as equal from the point of view of the soul even though differences may be observed in dealing with them according to the *Varna* (caste) and *Ashrama* (order) to which they belong, just as one uses the limbs of his own body differently.

36. **Absence of Egoism**—refers to absence of the feeling of 'I' in respect of the body, mind and intellect. And of the sense of doer ship in respect of actions performed by them.

37. **Friendliness (Universal Love)**—It consists in extending the feeling of love towards all creative, whether high or low.

38. **Charity**—consists in gratuitously supplying that which is needed in a particular place, at a particular time and by a particular person, gladly and respectfully, without expecting any return or reward.

39. **Devotion to Duty**—It includes values like 'sincerity' 'integrity' 'honesty;, 'loyalty to duty' etc. contained in the list of 83 values given in NCERT booklet.

40. **Tranquility**—This state if attained when the mind is completely free from desires and is peaceful, contended and perspicuous.

These are traditional values inherited from past, some of these values like non-accumulation of things', contentment and dispassion are practicable for saintly persons only. We may say that they are too righteous to cultivate in the individuals of this space-age for want of sufficient exemplary situations in the present set-up of the society.

Eighty-Three Values published by NCERT

The following is the list of 83 values given in NCERT

1. Abstinence
2. Appreciation of cultural values of others
3. Anti-touchability
4. Citizenship
5. Consideration for others
6. Concern for others
7. Cooperation
8. Cleanliness
9. Compassion
10. Common cause
11. Common good
12. Courage
13. Courtesy
14. Curiosity
15. Democratic decision making
16. Devotion
17. Dignity of the individual
18. Dignity of manual work
19. Duty
20. Discipline
21. Endurance
22. Equality
23. Friendship
24. Faithfulness
25. Fellow-feeling
26. Freedom
27. Forward look
28. Good manner
29. Gentlemanliness
30. Gratitude
31. Honesty
32. Helpfulness
33. Humanisn
34. Hygienic living
35. Initiative
36. Integrity
37. Justice

38. Kindness
39. Kindness to animals
40. Loyalty to duty
41. Leadership
42. National Unity
43. National consciousness
44. Non-violence
45. National integration
46. Obedience
47. Peace
48. Proper utilization of time
49. Punctuality
50. Patriotism
51. Purity
52. Quest for knowledge
53. Resourcefulness
54. Regularity
55. Respect for others
56. Reverence for old age
57. Sincerity
58. Simple living
59. Social justice
60. Self-discipline
61. Self-help
62. Self-respect
63. Self-confidence
64. Self-support
65. Self-study
66. Self-reliance
67. Self-control
68. Self-restraint
69. Social service
70. Solidarity of mankind
71. Sense of discrimination between good and bad
72. Sence of social responsibility
73. Socialism
74. Sympathy
75. Secularism and respect for all religions
76. Spirit of enquiry
77. Team work
78. Team spirit
79. Truthfulness
80. Tolerance
81. Universal truth
82. Universal love
83. Value for national and civic property

publication styled as "*Documents on Social, Moral and Spiritual Values*". Shri B.R. Goel, the compiler, claims that the list has been compiled on the basis of documents included in the publication as well as a study of the Gandhian Literature.

In the list of above values there is repetition as well as overlapping of purpose conveyed by certain values. For example we can take a few values from the above list—self-confidence and self-reliance, self-control and self-restraint, tolerance and endurance, concern for others and consideration for other, kindness and kindness to animals. National unity and National integration, common cause and common good. In fact, owing to complex nature of human feeling, psycho-cultural bent of mind, divergent individual and social differences there cannot be regimentation of words sounding different values. Therefore, there is no fixed or exact number of values nor can there be any exhaustive list of values. In the above list even the number being as high as 83 a few important values like co-existence, preservation of culture and natural environment etc. are missing. One may argue that this value (co-existence) is connotated by other values like, universal love already included in the list. This argument may stand the test of brevity. With the brevity point of view the list may be incorporated under the following six subheads:

1. **Righteousness**—Abstinence, cleanliness, compassion, common cause, common good, cooperation, courage, courtesy, discipline, endurance, friendship, faithfulness, good manners, hygienic living, justice, obedience, proper utilization of time, purity, quest for knowledge, simple living, self-help, self-study, self-reliance, self-support, self-confidence, self-respect, sympathy, sense of discrimination between good and bad, truthfulness, tolerance.

2. **Self-Discipline**—Forward looking, self-control, self-restraint, punctuality, regularity, honesty, sincerity, loyalty to duty, integrity, initiative, resourcefulness.
3. **Fellow feeling**—Helpfulness, concern for others, respect for others, reverence for old age.
4. **Humanism**—Consideration for others, concern for others, curiosity, dignity of the individual, dignity of manual work, gentlemanliness, gratitude, social-service, solidarity of mankind, sense of social responsibility, spirit of enquiry, team-work, team spirit.
5. **Democratic sense**—Citizenship, democratic decision making, equality, freedom, leadership, national unity, national consciousness, patriotism, social justice, socialism, value for national and civic property.
6. **Non-violence**—Appreciation of cultural values, antiuntouchability, kindness, kindness to animals, secularism and respect for all religions, universal truth, universal love.

According to a section of educationists search for new human values, which would be more consonant with the global consciousness of our times and responsive to the changes brought about by science and technology and to the urgency of wide-scale problems being faced by mankind are suggested.

Dr. Prem Kirpal, former Secretary of Education, Government of India has rightly pointed out that "the charter of the United Nations, the Constitution of UNESCO and the Declaration of Human Rights embodied statements, principles and norms for the observance by the member states are very conducive to the evolution of proper human values that can be practiced and shared by all in the making of a new humanism for the emerging global community". In this context he has mentioned the following value concepts:

1. Man and his own self: the human person, the inner man.
2. Man and his fellowmen: society: human relations
3. Man and his habitac:Natural; space
4. Man and his work
5. Man and his art
6. Man and Technology
7. Man and his Technology
8. Man and time:The stream of past, present and future.
9. Man and his cosmos (Man and his universe; the meaning and purpose of existence).

Beside these traditional and modern value concepts mostly applicable to the individual there are a few values to be observed by societies and nations for the harmonious growth of human being and global peace. Some of such value-concepts have been enumerated in the declaration of Congress for Human Unity held at Philadelphia in May, 1976. They are as following:

A. Compassionate love.
B. Intrinsic worth of each human being.
C. Right for all people to develop their creativity.
D. The inter-dependence of all nations.
E. Solidarity.
F. Freedom and justice for all people.
G. Complete disarmament.
H. Decentralization of power.
I. Freedom of expression of thought.
J. The right to work for just rewards.

K. Preservation of natural and cultural environments.

L. The adjustment of economic structures for greater equality and justice for people.

M. Abolition of all forms of slavery, torture and capital punishment.

To inculcate these values among the people some high level decisions are to be taken. Authority is exercised and bills are passed by the competent bodies, if necessary.This explains why they are called global values, national values and so on whereas to cultivate the value concepts stated earlier personal influence, experience and several other strategies are used. As per the new approach of value education no pressures are to be used, rather more situations for clarification of values and free choices are to be provided. Under the sub-head 'Methodology' we will discuss here itself a few modes and methods of internalization of these value-concepts.

Classification of Values

1. **Academic values**—like regularity and devotion in teaching, impartiality in assessment, honesty and integrity in research and publication, healthy competition and objectivity, search for excellence and originality.

2. **Moral values**—like honesty, integrity, sense of responsibility and compassion. The realm of moral values is rather a debatable one.

3. **Socio-political values**—like national integration and international understanding, society vs. individual, social responsibility and citizenship, democracy and humanism. These are the values required for the survival of a socio-political system. The difference between moral values and socio-political values is very subtle. Among all socio-political values national

integration is of utmost importance particularly for teachers.

4. **Scientific temper**—objectivity, rationalism, fact-base and investigative approach, looking into the hows and whys of problems.
5. **Global values**—consist of all those values pertinent and significant for global peace and order, solidarity, freedom and justice for all, complete disarmament, abolition of all forms of slavery, torture and capital punishment etc. can be numerated under this sub-heading.
6. **Human rights**—consist of all the rights scripted to the all citizens
7. **Environmental values**—consist of preservation of natural environment, forestation, awareness and concern towards pollution etc.
8. **Cultural values**—Cultural unity, respect for other's culture, preservation of culture etc. Although we speak of the culture of a group, or of a country the essence of cultural elements in individual help to make for cultural unity, for functional group interaction and for organised, purposeful living together. Differences in cultural elements among individuals and conflict in values and purposes within individuals, often lead to tensions and to change in cultural characteristics and values.

Principles of Value Based Education in the Indian Constitution

The Constitution is the mirror of desires, ambitions, ideals and values of a country. The Indian Constitution is a vast document. Moral values and civic-sense have been described at many places in the Constitution. First of all the values have been showed in the preamble of the Constitution.

Preamble of Constitution: The aim of our constitution has been described in the preamble. It includes the principle of moral values and civic-sense.

Justice social, economic and political; liberty of thought expression, belief, faith and worship; equality of status and opportunity; fraternity of the dignity of individual and unity and integrity of the nation.

Besides, socialism, secularism and democracy have been included in it.

1) **Sovereignty:** People have the ultimate power to elect their government and government is accountable and responsible to people. A parliamentary democracy and republic organisation was needed whose responsibility was to work for the welfare of the people and providing the values mentioned in the Constitution preamble article 38(1), 75(3), 164(2) and 326.
2) **Socialism:** The meaning of socialism is equality of social, economic and political justice (preamble, article 38, and 39). Following the objective of equality, policy to eradicate all types of explanation in the society to be adopted.
3) **Secularism:** Secularism implies equal status to every religion. The constitution did not setup a state religion. It guaranteed equality of treatment of all religion *(Sarva dharma sambhav)* and protection of religious right of minorities. Secularism has been an integral part of Indian society (Preamble, article 25-26, 29-30, 44, 51A)
4) **Justice:** It is responsibility of any government to provide socio-economic and political justice to all without any discrimination. The Government should develop such a social, economic system in which all people are provided justice without any discrimination. Fundamental principle have been given in the form of

directive principle of state policies of the constitution. There is provision of a socio-economic programme for the development of economic democracy which form the objectives and foundation of political democracy. These Directive Principles of State Policy (DPSP) are national objectives. The DPSP act as guidelines to setup the welfare state and reflect national awareness and ambition of freedom fighters of our national movement.

5) **Liberty:** The concept liberty of thought, expression, belief, faith and worship is indispensable for a democratic state. The very concept has been included in the fundamental rights. These fundamental rights are justifiable. And they are considered essential for the development of the people and the nation. Provision of liberty for Indian citizen is really very a progressive step (preamble and article 12 to 35).

Essential human rights have been included in the fundamental rights so that the fundamental human values of the dignity of person may be protected and fostered for a better life. And only a true and democratic rule can guarantee these rights. There should be reasonable restrictions on personal liberty because these freedoms are the basis of a citizen's moral, social and political life.

In Unnikrishnan's case (AIR 1993) the Supreme Court said that the right to education is included in the right to live. Emphasising the importance of education for a person to live, the Supreme Court expressed belief in the *Niti Shatak* written in 1st century B.C, in which great scholar Bhatrihari had said "A person without education is like an animal". (*Vidhyavihin Pashu*)

Right to Liberty and Educational Value

Explaining the right to liberty (Article 21) the honorable Supreme Court said in an important decision that the right to liberty is linked with dignity of a person i.e. right to dignified life. Dignity of person is incomplete without education. Since education is high moral value, it should be inculcated and included as a fundamental right.

1) **Equality**: All the citizens have equal rights without any discrimination. Equality has social, political, economic and legal aspects. Its connotative meaning is equality of status and, opportunity to enjoy right in socio-economic and political life and activity and participation without any discrimination on ground of race, religion, caste, sex, place of birth or any of them.

   All the people enjoy equality before law, equal protection of law and equal opportunity (preamble, article 14-18).

2) **Fraternity:** The concept of common brotherhood and Indian joint families creates ideals of freedom, equality and fraternity. All the more important in the context of need for strengthening the feelings of fraternity and friendship in a multidiversified society. The importance of principle of fraternity lies in fostering the feeling of harmony, conciliation, unity and unison in Indian people and other people because this feeling overcomes all type of religious, linguistic, caste and provincial or class differences. The concept of *Vasudaiva Kutumbkum* has been materialized i.e. the whole world is a single family. The objective of fraternity have been included in the preamble of the society and now it has been included in Article 51(5) of the constitution.

3) **Unity and Integrity of the Nation:** The unity and integrity of nation lies in strong bond of patriotism and national feeling. Diversity and unity is a characteristic feature of our nation. Nationality, unity and integrity of the nation is the foundation of our constitution. Without the above unique features, our nation and its constitution is meaningless. There is harmony between unity and diversity. It is not only between unity and

diversity of India, but also between social groups, subnationalties, individuals, government and private system of local institution.

The aforesaid basic constitutional values and its standard the were long cherished dreams of the founding fathers of our constitution, whose utmost purpose was to build a unified modern and democratic nation-state. These constitutional values provide guidelines of moral values and civic-sense related to the values and responsibilities of citizens.

Citizen's Values and Fundamental Duties in the Context of Value Based Education

Success and qualitativeness of a democratic state completely depends on quality, characters, truthfulness, discipline, thoughts and values and moral and legal commitment towards fundamental duties of the citizens i.e. the citizens are the rulers of the country and subjects as well. Citizens are residents of India who have some right and who have created the Indian democracy and provided themselves a constitution to control the smooth functioning of the nation-state. These citizens are rulers and people of state. As a unit of Indian democracy, Indian-citizens enjoy all the rights and manage all its institutions. Citizens have civil, political, economic and constitutional rights, responsibilities fundamental duties which can be considered a part of civic-sense. As a voter or public employee or as a member of a community, who is involved in various routine activities, a citizen plays powerful role by following personal, commercial and human or moral values. On the basis of these possible means these values makes a person aware of his capability to reach great heights by following his duties honestly. It is thus essential for every citizen to have and work with high ideals and with more responsibility to enable

India become strong socially, economically and politically. School has to undertake special responsibility in this regard.

The basic values and fundamental duties are clear order of morality and these orders have been conferred by the constitution. These values urges the Indian citizens to sink narrow differences and self interest. So that we may work to attain the national income wellbeing and welfare of co-citizen.

Citizens are the main focus point of socio-economic development of society and nations. Thus positive and constructive citizenship is the back-bone of any society. Some values are equal in all circumstances for good citizenship in any democracy; Many civil, political, economic, cultural right attainments and active participation in social life for taking valuable self decision and enhancing social welfare. It implies that one should accept duties and responsibility towards one's country, co-citizen and society.

Liberty, equality, fraternity are basic traditions and values of a democracy so these rights are unbreakably directly and indirectly related to duties and responsibilities. As a whole, fundamental values of citizenship in a Constitution can be explained as follows.

- To use their valuable voting rights freely and properly to elect truthful and good-character representatives who are committed to their party manifesto and active co-operation in public works.
- To make policies and take decision for well-being of the people and help in creating consensus. Representatives should respect and tolerate different views and opinions.

Citizens of any republic state have to accept those responsibilities which are basically moral. Theoretically it can be argued that fundamental rights mentioned in the Indian Constitution are also followed by some duties. A famous American thinker Walter Lipman argued that every right you wish for has duties which you have to fulfil.

Fundamental duties have been given in Article 51 A of the Indian Constitution which have following values of citizenship.

- To abide by the constitution and respect its ideals and institutions, the National flag and National Anthem;
- To cherish and follow the noble ideals which inspired our national struggle for freedom;
- To uphold and protect the sovereignty, unity and integrity of India;
- To defend the country and render national service when called upon to do so;
- To promote harmony and the spirit of common brotherhood amongst all the people of India transcending religious, linguistic and regional or sectional diversities; to renounce practices derogatory to the dignity of women;
- To value and preserve the rich heritage of our composite culture;
- To protect and improve the natural environment including forests, lakes, rivers and wildlife and to have compassion for living;
- To develop the scientific temper, humanism and the spirit of inquiry and reform;
- To safeguard public property and to abjure violence;
- To strive towards excellence in all spheres of individual and collective activity so that the nation constantly rise to higher levels of endeavour and achievement.

These fundamental duties of citizens to nation express great ideals, moral-values and value education.

Justice J. S. Verma Committee which was setup for fundamental duties of the citizen expounded principles which are applicable in all aspects of public life:

- **Selfishness:** Government officers should take decision only for the wellbeing of the people. They should not take decisions for themselves, their family or to get their friends, financial or any other material benefit.
- **Truthfulness:** Government official should not accept any type of bribery or gratitude from unknown persons or institution which affect the performance of his duties and post.
- **Objectivity:** During government service, at the time of selection of candidates, agreement and appropriate candidates on the basis of eligibility without any prejudice.
- **Accountability:** Government officials are accountable towards people for their decisions and deeds and they should accept probes regarding their post.
- **Transparency:** Decisions and work of government officers should be transparent as far as possible. They should give causes for taking decisions and any information should be hidden only when it is necessary for national interest or well-being of the people.
- **Honesty:** It is the duty of government officials that they should make declarations of their own interests regarding government work and solve the created problem in the favour of public interest.
- **Leadership:** Government officials should promote and support these principles by their leadership and become role models.

Analysis of Different Education Commissions, Committees and other Documents in Context of Value Based Education.

1. University Education Commission (1948-49)

University Education Commission which was constituted under presidency of Dr. Sarvapalli Radhakrishnan, said Value-based education is best. Earlier, teachers and teaching used to emphasise on inculcation of wisdom, but now-a-days it is gradually declining and has been confined to mere information. The commission has written "Where is the wisdom we have lost in knowledge? Where is the knowledge we have lost in information." The commission has also said, "We cannot protect freedom until and unless we protect the values like justice, liberty, equality, fraternity. We can get freedom only when we have feeling of equality for deprived and poor people, good feeling towards women believe in fraternity without discrimination on the ground of religion, creed, caste, sex, place of birth, and maintain peace and harmony. The main goal of education is character building. Universities will have to inculcate discipline in the students and their energy should be used for constructive works. Students should be given training for democracy, some basic values like fearlessness, concentration and strong-determination should be developed." According to Dr. Radhakhrishnan, education is an important tool for national unity through which right outlook can be developed in the persons.

1) **School Level:** The suggestions of the commission at school level, specially at middle school level are as follows:

   i) Students should be taught good stories based on morality and religious principles.

   ii) Students should be taught biographies of great peronalities.

iii) Great achievements and good opinion of geat personalities should be included in the biographies.

(iv) Stories and biographies should be published with reverence and in a good manner.

2) **At University Level:** At university level, the goal of education should be to inculcate moral and spiritual education. Universities should create power of knowledge in students which may help in the promotion of education to make democracy a success, search for knowledge continuously, and know the meaning and gist of human life.

All educational institutes should start their routine work after silent meditation of some minutes.

In the first year of the degree courses students should be taught biographies of great leaders of world Lord Budha, Confusious, Socrates, Lord Christ, Shankar, Ramanujan, Madhav, Muhamad Sahib, Kabir, Nanak and Gandhi.

In the second year, students should be taught selective part of scriptures of universal importance.

In the third year, students should be taught the important features of religion and philosophy.

2. Secondary Education Commission (1952-53)

According to suggestions of the secondary education commission, value education will have to be made the base of education. The commission writes in this regard. India has achieved political freedom recently and declared itself a secular republic state after enough discussion. Therefore, education should develop these tendencies and characteristics in the citizens through which they may fulfil the responsibilities of citizenship very well and prevent those disintegrating tendencies which are helpful from wide national secular outlook.

The aim of secondary education is to train the youth of the country to be good citizens who will be play their part effectively in the social reconstruction and economic development of their country.

Explaining their goals and aims of secondary education, the commission explained the goals of education which includes, inculcation of republic citizenship. The commission is of the opinion that since India is an independent nation and its goal is to establish a secular republic, citizens should be trained according to new environment of India. Traits like good opinion, clarity in speech and writing, cleanliness, socialistic discipline, co-operation, tolerance, true patriotism, world citizenship are necessary to develop in the citizens. It can be achieved through school teaching. Teaching method should not only inculcate knowledge but also desirable values, proper attitude and working habits in the students. Character building is the special responsibility of the teachers. So education of character building should be given in every programme of the school. A true patriotism and tolerance should be inculcated in the students. They should know dignity of labour and develop the working habits. Students should be given training of discipline which may develop characteristic of leadership. Students should understand the cultural heritage and have knowledge of social value. All these above qualities and values were considered goals of secondary education.

3. Sri Prakash Committee (Suggestions of religious and moral education committee) 1959

The Government of India setup a committee on religious and moral institutions under presidency of Sri Prakash in August 1959. This committee presented its report before the government in 1960. The committee accepted that religious and moral education is neglected due to faulty education system. Value-education is necessary to make students, a good citizen and of good character.

The committee has expressed its views regarding the religious and value-education.

A) **At all levels of education:** The committee's recommendations from primary to universities level are as follows:

   i) Students should be taught comparative education of all basic religious views.

   ii) Students should be taught the gist of biographies of great leaders of religious importance.

   iii) As the students are mentally developed they should be introduced to moral, philosophical and spiritual principles.

   iv) Religious and moral books should be availed for students from primary to universities level.

B) **At Primary Level:** The committee's recommendations for primary level are as follows:

   i) The urge to serve should be developed in the students.

   ii) Moral education should be provided to the students in two periods a week.

   iii) Students should be taught simple and interesting stories which are related to saints and religious thinkers.

C) **At Secondary Level:** The committees recommendations for secondary level are as follows.

   i) Students should be taught important principles of great religions of the world.

   ii) In holidays and after school hours social-service groups should be orgaized develop the feeling of social service in the students as co-curricular activities.

D) **At University Level:** The committee's recommendations are as follows:

i) General studies of various religions should be made a compulsory part of syllabus of the degree course.

ii) In the first and second year of the degree course religious and sacred books should be taught.

iii) Comparative study of religions should be at post graduate level.

The gist of Sri Prakash committee suggestions is that the value-education related to students character and ethics should be given in school in place of homes. This education should develop right and factual outlook in the children towards values. The committee considered education as a requirement of moral and character development.

4. The National Education Commission (1964-66):

National Education Commission has written— "India is in a unique position because it has a great tradition of non attachment, tolerance, peace loving, compassion to living... many a time these precious things had been forgotten and we were entangled in passionism, malaise and tendency of harmful criticism. The need of the hour is to start a new campaign and express deep faith to live high ideals of peace, freedom, truth and compassion."

"Education is an important component of social faith and political transformation so we will have to see it as national desires. Education and National development are complementary. The efforts for pluralistic democracy, equalitarian society is possible through change in education so the entire education should internally be transformed. Social, moral and spiritual values and self discipline can be enriched with the help of education. Moral and spiritual values can be developed by making moral teachings of various religions apart from education."

The commission stated, "It is but natural to have great expectations from our classrooms; our teachers and students very often fall short of our expectations because their personalities are developed mostly by assimilating and vomiting of the information (knowledge) and not by acquisition of moral and spiritual values. The gap between the content and the living experience of its pupils between, the system of values that it preaches and the goals setup by the society, between the ancient curriculum and the modernity of science is making the situation worse. The changing of curriculum is such that students find it difficult to cope up with the burden of the curriculum. Parental expectations are also very high."

A serious defect in the school curriculum is the absence of provision of education in social, moral and spiritual values. For majority of Indians, religion is a great motivational force and is intimately involved in the formation of character and the inculcation of ethical values.

The National System of education that is related to life needs and aspiration of the people cannot afford to ignore this purposeful force. We recommend, therefore, that conscious and organised attempts be made imparting education in social, moral and spiritual values.

According to Education Commission (1964-66) the main goals of education is education of moral and spiritual values. The commission accepted that religion is the great inspirational power. Religion is the basis of evalution of moral value and character building. Thus, there should be a combined effort to educate by spiritual values and social and moral education of great religions. The commission has realised the need for formal education of these values. According to the commission moral education should be provided to the students one or two hours a week. There should be an effort to giving shape with every aspects of student's moral life. The National Education Commission (1964-66) has accepted that the absence of moral and spiritual values is a big fault in school's curricula. If we eliminate moral education and spiritual thinking from our educational institutes we will then be working against complete historical development.

The commission has said the value based education is the necessity of democracy and expressed the following view.

School level: For school level the commission's suggestions are as follows:

(1) Students should be taught basic moral, social and spiritual values viz. truth, honesty, social responsibility, compassion, tolerance, respect for the aged, sympathy for the poor etc.

(2) Aforesaid values to be made an integral part of school programmes.

(3) To educate for the aforesaid values, few hours a week to be set aside in the time table.

(4) All religions of the world should be given proper place in the school syllabus.

(5) For the whole country, similar books for the same subject should be prepared on national level by religious experts.

(6) At primary level, basic values and life related problems should be taught from the selective stories of great religions of India and world.

(7) At secondary level aforesaid problems and values should be considered by teachers and students.

(8) The story of great religious and spiritual leaders should be taught in higher classes of secondary level.

(9) The main problems of great religions of world should be studied in the last two years at secondary level.

University Level: The commission's suggestions at university level are as follows:

i) Students should be taught respect, equality, social justice, welfare state etc.

ii) To inculcate moral, social and spiritual values in students, materials to be collected from cultures of other country.

iii) General study of various religions of the world should be included in first year degree course syllabus.

iv) Biographies of great religious leaders should be taught in first year of degree course.

v) In the second year of degree course students should be taught about universally important people from religious books of the world.

vi) In third year of degree course the main problems of philosophy of religion should be studied thoroughly.

vii) Proper religious and moral literature should be prepared by labour department of the universities.

5. National Education Policy (1986)

In the national education policies, concern over declination of fundamental values and increasing disbelief has been expressed. The policy has laid emphasis on including these values in the syllabus so that education may become a powerful means of social and moral values. Indian cultural multiplicity was accepted in it and it has been said, "Education should develop universal and eternal value in the interest of unity and integrity of our people". The powerful role of education in eliminating conservatism, fanatism, violence, surerstitious and has been defined in the policy.

Besides, it has been said that our heritage was in emphasizing national aim and universal value and the positive role of value based education.

The National Education Policy was constituted in 1986. According to create a Policy value education has been accepted as an important part of education and responsibility. Regarding this, the basic principles of our National Education Policy are as follows:

1) Education for all.
2) Education makes a person cultured. It should sharpen our sensitivity to increase scientific understanding to make habit of scientific thinking, to prove national unity, it should be helpful in harnessing socialism, secularism and democracy which is mentioned in the constitution.
3) Education should be the basis of self-dependence of a person and nation. It should develop manpower at every stage so as to enable one meet economic needs.
4) Education should improve the present and make the future attractive.
5) To change the bookish pattern of education.
6) To create a feeling of social responsibility of education.
7) Education as a part of social change in 21st century.
8) Technological view to be adopted in education.
9) To inculate character, moral, spiritual values along with scientific temperament in students.
10) To create awareness towards social and economic atmosphere.

On the basis of these principles, the basic mantra of National Education Policy is that, at a certain level, all students should be provided good and similar education without any discrimination on the basis of religion, race, caste, creed, sex, place of birth. In the single part from national education curriculum necessary elements related to history of Indian freedom struggle, constitutional responsibility, national dignity will be included and these topics will be covered in all subjects. In so doing, so national values like our cultural heritage, democracy, secularism, social equality, gender equality, ideals of small family, development of scientific temper will become part of our lives. Although birth and social environment of particular family is a coincidence even then traditional values creates frustration and prejudice in our minds. To remove them is the goal of national education system so that minimum education standard will be required. Such step should be taken so that students can understand the cultural tradition and social system of different parts of the country. Emphasis should be given to eliminate poverty, national unity, ideals of small family, equality of men, working knowledge and development of skill etc.

It is clearly mentioned in National Education Policy that value education should not be confined to the classroom and to the syllabus. Establishment of link between school and community and community singing of folk songs should be a part of curriculum. The basic reason behind this process is to shape the values in the form of conduct and behaviour.

6. Programme of Action (1986)

In the action plan of National Education Policy special attention has been given to work-list of education like moral-values and civic-sense. For complete education up to secondary level all aspects of education are widely described. In this, value based education is emphasised as an indispensable or integral part of school curriculum. According to this document the main objectives are as follows.

(a) To develop and make student's understanding more

intense about socio-economic and political development and the rich culture of free India as an independent nation.

(b) To develop student's understanding about current problems such as international peace, human right and establishment of a just world system in global context.

(c) To develop innovative mind, scientific temper and farsightedness against injustice and *Ponga panth* (odious religious practice). The aim of art education is to foster aesthetism and develop knowledge and understanding about cultural heritage.

In the action plan, work experience has been presumed as a part of learning process and purposeful physical work. It should produce such service useful for community and this education should be basic which is component at all levels of education. In addition to it, emphasis has been laid on the development of respect for physical work, manual work, self- reliance, co-operation, tolerance, helping others, curiosity, work-morality, productive work related inclination and values and concern for the community.

7. Aacharya Rammurti Committee (1990)

This committee reviewed the national education policy. The tittle of the policy's report was "Towards an enlightened and human society." This committee stressed that education should provide an atmosphere for the establishment of values. The Rammurti Report has accepted the necessity of value for the progress of the society and has expressed worry about decline of moral-values— when we look towards our great civilisation and heritage, this tendency acquires a special meaning. It is the responsibility of our educational institutes to work with deep concern and intelligence in these circumstances of this wide massive decline in values so that they (educational institutions, may aslo play an important role in the value-education. This task cannot be done by organising special classes, studying the text-books mechanically, through delivering lectures or cramming method. In fact, value education should develop in an integral form of the entire teaching process and school atmosphere. The values like democracy, secularism, socialism, scientific outlook, equality of sex, honesty, faithfulness, courage and justice and respect for all creatures and different cultures and languages etc. build the base for such values which are basic for the unity and integrity of the nation. If these basic values are not included in the education process, education will lose its inherent importance and essence. All the syllabus based and curricular activities of the school and colleges should be organised with determination. This report enables us to understand that a person has an important role in society and he should know his right as well as his duties so that he is not only aware of his rights but also of his duties.

8. Yashpal Committee (1991)

Yashpal committee suggested that every school should make organised efforts for the development of some essential qualities in all the children which have been discussed below. These qualities are those basic values which will contribute in personal, social and national development in the long run.

(i) Regularity and Punctuality:

These values are expressed in sensitivity towards value of time and punctuality. Their importance in every walk of life and in progress is widely known. For example, children are to learn such habits or life styles by which the regularity of going to school daily and in time becomes a part of their natural behaviour and they are affected by outside control or pressure.

It is the reponsibility of our educational institutes to work with deep concern and intelligence in these circumstances of this wide massive decline in values.

(ii) Cleanliness:

Cleanliness is such tendency which a person learns towards his atmosphere. This value is expressed in the form of a child's personal habit of leading a healthy life and keeping himself and his closest physical environment neat and clean. Clearly there are other qualities which are directly linked with those learning experience of the children which are provided to them in their early school and home life.

(iii) Importance of Manual Work:

It is not as much related to those specific behaviours of the children as much it is related to those values which they associate with the attainment of the goal through hardwork and labour. The development of this value prepares the children to take the responsibility of goal oriented work, execute them with patience and finish them in time.

(iv) Duty and Urge to Serve:

These values are expressed in the form of devotion of sacrificing selfishness for the welfare of others without any fear or bias. It implies developing sympathy in children towards their neighbours, mates and companions, handicapped, the aged etc. and the devotion of providing help voluntarily.

(v) Equality:

This oath should be accepted that all are equal even after the differences on the grounds of caste, creed, religion or sex. It is necessary to develop the tendency in the children of looking at theirs and others relationships in equalitarian context. This outlook should be developed in every child through school experience so that he may grow up as such an adult who considers himself a part of equal people's community. In the community every member has some common rights, responsibilities and duties towards the society. The final aim of equality is to help children to progress towards a world scenario that is free from linguistic, regional, cultural, religious, social and economic discrimination.

(vi) Co-operation:

This value of attaining the common goal together can be inculcated in the children by working together in and outside the school and providing opportunities for working. Children should be able to understand the need for co-operative efforts. For it they should be first made to understand the natural mutual dependence of human beings at local, national and international levels. This work should undoubtedly be done with great care so that the feeling of self-dependence, personality and competition in the children may not be enclongered which are equally important.

(vii) Responsibility:

The responsibility in children refers to devotion of facing difficulties and problems with commitments and faith while performing various tasks. Self-confidence on individual capabilities and positive-image of one's self should be developed in the children.

(viii) Truthfulness:

Truthfulness in one's behaviour in every aspect of work and life is every person's basic inspiration. Its wide importance lies in determining the behaviour of children and it makes his every behaviour valid. It is imperative to guide children properly in school and at homes and help them to develop the will power of translating their thoughts into action and behaviour.

(ix) Nationality oneness:

The children should learn to feel oneness with the nation.

It should be long and similar process which may develop respect and willingness in the children to protect fundamental values, establishment in the constitution and respect for national emblems.

(A) Development of Specified Values:

The development of specified cognitive abilities can often be linked with various specified fields of school curriculum. But this does not apply to the development of values of uncognitive field. It is not possible to relate the specified goal with some special field or subject learning. It's more appropriate to say that they are directly or indirectly related to every learning experience of the school. Although the school will always be in high colours from values development point of view, family and community will keep playing important roles in it. They will help children differentiate those values and make them a part of their personal lifestyle. It makes the noncognitive work of the school, complex and difficult. Some suggestions have been given about schools, parents and communities role which help children to attain basic values during primary education period.

(B) The Role of School:

School is a place where children start working after thinking a lot, where behaviour and knowledge are reflected in conduct. Children develop tendencies, tastes liking and disliking, persons, issues and problems which they have to face in their life. Thus the qualification of the students depend on the inputs of curriculum and their use in school. The school should organise learning experience in such a way that children may attain cognitive and incognitive qualifications in a balanced manner. It is often said that cognitive goals elmininate school activities and no attention is paid to affective goals. It is important to make planned efforts to organise those learning experience which may not leave any place for doubt in the attainment of minimum results in affective and psychomotor area.

As far as special role of the school is the noncognitive qualification development process, we should pay attention to four important aspects.

(i) School Organisation:

Children learn values like faith, cleanliness, the urge to serve, co-operation informally in the school's closest environment to a large extent so it becomes indispensable that these values clearly reflect in various school activities, the way of physical organisation and its maintenance. For example, if school environment is not clean or there is discrimination among girls and boys during organising school activities, then there are less responsibilities that students will learn—the value of cleanliness and man-woman equality. Thus, the present requirement is to give maximum attention to organisational structure, physical system and learning activities. It will make school by and large an effective instrument in helping the uncognitive field's value development.

(ii) Teacher :

It is a universal fact that children learn emotional values by seeing their elders' behaviour and by following them. Willingly or unwillingly the teacher is an ideal role-model which students have tendency to follow in their early life. So, it becomes the serious responsibilitiy of every teacher in matters such as how he presents himself as human being, his/her tendencies, working habits and life styles he does not only see as knowledge and efficiency given but also as the inner and outer children's tendencies of personal behaviour in and outside the class.

(iii) Curriculum Inputs:

Though noncognitive qualification of emotional fields are not taught to a large extent, the role of learning experience of various fields is important. In forming the tendencies and tastes of children it is necessary to select and direct curriculum inputs in the class with great care and in an appropriate manner. For example, wrongly selected language lessons may develop cognitive abilities, but they may inspire undesired linguistic, regional tendencies in the children. Similarly, wrongly selected and taught contexts of social studies may inculcate partition thoughts in the children in place of patriotism. Similarly, the basis of appropriate knowledge make the development of proper tendency towards environment and personal health. While selecting curriculum experience, we should not only pay attention to cognitive capabilities but also to various noncognitive capabilities of the children.

(iv) Physical Education, Work-experience and Arts Education

Although the attainment of results of noncognitive fields is also possible through determined activities of environmental studies, even then cognitive results are often emphasised in these subjects. On the contrary, there are more opportunities of flexibility, freedom of organising functions and expressions of naturalness and creativity. There are greater possibilities of the attainment of results of noncognitive field through them. These fields provide children opportunities of freely inquiring, experiencing and indulging in mutual activities with their physical and social environment and help in values, development viz. natural respect and co-operation, dignity of labour, realisation of achievements and identity, etc. It is a matter of regret that schools have been paying much less attention towards uncognitive fields learning experience due to ever increasing burden of syllabus in academic subjects, books-oriented and exam-oriented teaching. It is necessary to change this tendency and ensure that these fields are given a just place in school curriculum/annual calendar.

(v) Curricular activities

In every education programme of the first level, there should be enough possibilities of organising various curricular activities and experiences besides various determined syllabus activities. These activities provide lot of opportunities for the development of various personal and social values to work on determined curricular inputs without any boundation. It is a matter of regret that very little importance is given to hidden possibilities in curricular activities for attainment of all-round development of children at primary level.

(C) The Role of Parents and Community

As it has been mentioned earlier also that emotional field's learning results can not directly be linked with any specific group which provide curriculum experience through formal process. These values continuously develop through schools in and outside sub sections. The role of parents at home and community is important in this informal learning process. In an ideal stage, home, community and school should play complementary and mutual energised roles. But it is not practically true. There are a large number of parents and community members who consider education and cognitive learning as one and do not care a bit about balanced personality development of children. It will be wrong to expect from a school specially in the context of noncognitive results attainment that a school should do not more than it can. This work should be seen as a joint responsibility of school, home and community. There is no way out and it should be our effort to help them to the maximum extent in mutual process for the attainment of this aim.

To foster learning in this aspect, school can play an active role. For example, Parents Teachers Association (PTA) can play an important role; long-lasting mutual relationship between parents, teachers and education administration of the area/region can be useful in making educational programme smooth to lay stress on noncognitive aspects of learning. These efforts should be multidimensional, these efforts will be energised which school is making for those ethics in which all the aspects will be stressed in a balanced manner in a place of the prevalent tradition of laying a lot more emphasis on congnitive results of learning.

National Curriculum Draft 2000

N.C.E.R.T. has prepared the National Curriculum Draft. It has various principles of moral-values and value education. After independence, essential social moral and spiritual values and virtues have been declining continuously for the last five decades. Malice and bitterness are increasing at all levels. Though schools are not untouched from the indifference towards atmosphere and disrespect for values has grown, their effective role and responsibility to give direction to the people of the nation cannot be undermined. Schools can and should make efforts to establish those universal and eternal values which make people progress towards unity and enable them feel and understand their moral and spiritual development. Such efforts should make them aware of the ability present in themselves. Value based education will co-operate in fighting against evils like bigotism, ill will, violence, dishonesty, corruption, exploitation and drug addiction. The recommendation of Justice J. S. Verma Committee about moral duties of the citizens pave the way for determination for fundamental human values and social justice. The arrangement made for including ten fundamental duties of the citizen is an important indication of the fact—regarding what a country expects from its citizens? All these things should be given a very important place in the entire school system all over India. Besides, the school should inculcate some important qualities such as—regularity and self-control, laboriousness, the urge to serve others, responsibility, diligence, creativity, sensitivity towards all, equality at large scale, fraternity, democratic outlook and faith in environmental protection. Therefore in the present context, personal, social, national and spiritual values—cleanliness and punctuality, good conduct, tolerance and justice, faith in national pride respect for law and order, truth, love and its continuity will have to be specially emphasized. Fundamental duties and the centred constituents of the curriculum and human rights will have to be included at all levels of school education in which children specially women's rights will be included.

— Enhance knowledge and respect for national emblems and inspire to express aspiration and determination towards ideals like national pride and unity.

— Create deep realization of patriotism and nationalism fired by the concept of *Vasudhaive Kutumbkam.*

— Inculcate personal, social, spiritual, moral, national values and other pertaining virtues which make a person effective from human and social point of view, make life meaningful and give direction to life.

(A) Education for Value-development :- A complete plan for value development was presented in the draft.

School Plan

Those principles should be inherent in the school curriculum which communicate essential values completely. Every activity, unit interactivity's examination, value-realisation, value-expansion, value-strength and then decisions to execute the values should be taken on the ground of balanced and proper work-policy. These values can be attained by clearly mentioning discipline which is developed by school goals, staff and student's participation. For accomplishment of values bilateral discussions, welfare services, help of the needy students, remedial-teaching, re-evaluation and the feeling of not discouraging students with less achievements are essential. For mention of such rules are essential which will ensure participation of every student in sports, school activities and their interests, programmes.

(i) **At Primary Level:**

a) School assembly, groups-songs and practice of silence and meditation.

b) Description of interesting stories and biographies associated with saints and holy scriptures.

c) The activities of the play ground i.e. sport. Such social service activities which create outlook of serving making alongwith other creature, even the nature and arouse the feeling of "work is worship".

d) Organisation of cultural programme and plays based on suitable topics and plots.

(ii) **Secondary and Higher Secondary Level:**

a) Guest lecturer citation and appropriate address of incidents knowledge, books and great literature in morning assemblies by the teachers.

b) Comparative study of essential teaching of main religions of the world and religious philosophers.

c) Social service in holidays and after school hours.

d) Group song programme, National Unity Camp, National social service and N.C.C. camp, scout and guiding programmes.

e) Cultural programmes, plays, symposiums etc. on appropriate topics.

Some schools may organise joint programmes to

celebrate important functions and festivals of all religions and cultural groups. It will develop understanding of one another, liking and respect feeling. A tolerant and well-organised society will be built.

(iii) **Complementary Co-operation:**

a) To mention the importance of inherent values in various subjects.

b) To provide the students opportunities of asking questions from one-another, partnership and respecting another.

c) To provide opportunities for democratic principles and process in class teaching.

d) To emphasise rise in man-woman equality, the feeling of equality towards social caste, classes and religious.

e) To demarcate the importance of human rights, rights of children, environmental protection, healthy life system etc.

f) To make the class environment tension free and democratic for the development of values.

(iv) Source of Value-Expansion:

a) Teachers should have clear outlook towards our role in value-consciousness.

b) Teachers should have the ability to recognize school subjects and conditions for nurturing universal values; they should be sensitive and aware of their self as role models of students.

c) Teachers should have understanding of resumptions and outlook of students.

d) They should make efforts honestly to attain goal for value education's teaching and class-management.

e) Teachers should develop positive attitude towards authorized and valid value awareness materiel for adopting various religions and values related to them in their life.

f) Teachers should be good communicators and messengers.

Universal Declaration of Human Responsibilities

(*Proposed by World Inter-Action Council, Vienna 1997)*

Preamble

The inborn dignity of all the members of all human families and their equal and untransferable rights' recognition is the foundation of freedom, justice and peace in the world. Duties and responsibilities are inherent in this while the result of emphasising rights may create clashes partition, unlimited dispute and quarrels. If we neglect human responsibilities, then disorder and chaos may in set in.

The rule of law and enrichment of human rights depend on man-woman's devotion to work properly. Worldwide problems need universal solution which can be achieved by such ideas, values and criterions as are respected by all culture and societies. It is the responsibilities of all people to encourage a better social-system in their countries and world according to their knowledge and abilities. Such a goal that cannot be attained by laws, instructions and convention.

While human aspiration of progress and reforms can be fulfilled by implementing approved values and criterions at all time and on all people and institution.

Now, therefore the General Assembly proclaims this Universal Declaration of Human Rights as a common standard of achievement for all people and all nations to the end that every individual and every organ of society keeping this declaration constantly in mind, shall strive by teaching and education to promote respect for their rights and freedom and by progressive measures, national and international to secure their universal rights and effect recognition and observance, both among the people of member, states themselves and among the people of territories under their jurisdiction.

Fundamental Principles for Mankind

Article – 1

It is the responsibility of every person to treat all people in a humane manner whatever his sex, racial origin, social status, political ideas, language, age, nationality may be.

Article – 2

No person should favour any kind of inhuman behaviour. Instead it is the responsibility of all the people to make efforts for other's dignity and self-respect.

Article – 3

No person, group or organization, state, military, or police is greater than goodness or evil; moral criterions are applied to all. It is the responsibility of every person to foster good and avoid evil.

Article – 4

All the logical–minded and conscious people should accept their responsibility towards each and every person, communities and families, the feeling of unity towards species, nations and religions: You should not do unto others as you don't wish to be done by.

Respect for non-violence and life

Article – 5

It is the responsibility of every person to respect life. No one has the right to hurt, torture or kill any other human-being. It does not snatch people's or communities' right to justified self-protection with you.

Article – 6

The disputes among states, group or people should be solved without violence. The Government should not tolerate massacre or terrorist activities nor should it participate in them. Neither should the government use womenfolk, children or any other civilian as a means of war. It is every citizen's and government official's responsibility to work peacefully and non-violently.

Article – 7

Every person is exceedingly important and he should be protected under any condition. No person or group should loot other person's or group's property nor should any person be deprived of his property.

Article – 9

It is the responsibility of all the people that they should make every possible effort to eradicate poverty, ignorance and inequality when necessary means are provided. They should foster conceptual development in the entire world.

Article – 10

It is the responsibility of all the people to develop their talents by making every possible effort. They should have equal opportunity to get education and purposeful work. Every person should help the needy, incapable persons and the victims of discrimination.

Article – 11

Entire property and wealth should be used strictly according to justice and for the progress of mankind. Economic and political power should not be used as a means of showing authority. Rather it should be used for economic justice and social system.

Truthfulness and Tolerance

Article – 12

It is the responsibility of every person to speak the truth and work honestly. However great or strong a person may be, he should not tell lies. The right to solitude and individual and professional secrecy should be respected. No person can be compelled to tell every person the entire truth at all times.

Article – 13

No politician, government employee, business leader, scientist, writer or artist is free from general moral codes. Nor are doctors, lawyers and other professionals free from these codes who have special duties towards their customers.

Article – 14

Media's freedom of informing the public and criticizing social institutions and government actions should be used with responsibility and demarcation. The responsibility of providing exact and true information is associated with media's freedom. Such complete news should not be given every time which may insult a person or lower his dignity.

Article – 15

Although people should be given the guarantee of religions freedom, it is the special responsibility of the religions representatives not to speak ill towards religions with different beliefs or indulge in discriminatory works. They should not infuriate hatred, bigotism and religions disputes. Rather they should encourage tolerance among people and respect towards one-another.

Mutual Respect and Participation

Article – 16

It is the responsibility of all men and women to show respect and intelligence towards one another in participation.

No person should exploit others sexually nor should he make him dependent on him. Rather sexual participants should accept the responsibility of each other's well-being.

Article – 17

Love, loyality and forgiveness in all our cultural and religions diversities and marriages and its purpose should be to guarantee safety and mutual help.

Article – 18

Family planning is every couple's responsibility. Mutual love, respect, understanding should be reflected in relationships between parents and children. No parent or other adult should exploit and misuse children nor should they misbehave with them.

Article – 19

No information in this declaration gives us the implication of any state, group or person acquiring such right that he may indulge in any activity or do any such work which aims at destroying any responsibility, right or freedom determined in this declaration or in the universal declaration of Human Rights.

Chapter-IV
Vision of Value Based Education

Introduction

The question of value based education is not an isolated one, its inter-links being closely associated to other sub-systems of our social set-up. Therefore, there cannot be any sure-shot or mechanical solution to the problems of value-education, as in its phenomena a cluster of opposites are involved i.e. emotion and reasoning, traditional curricula and modernity of science and technology, social behaviour patterns and actual learning experiences etc. But during the present decade our educationists and authorities have started to express their serious concern to the problem of deterioration of moral, social and spiritual values, which have been damaging well-knit fibres of our strong and valuable cultural canvas and creating hurdles in path of progress of the nation. Therefore, the concern to it has been expressed from several quarters. Thus value-oriented education is the crying need of the day, without which all our strategies may not work to fulfil the aspiration of the society for better education.

"It is being increasingly felt that no education can be complete or even worthwhile if it does not provide to the individual not only the knowledge of the history of moral, religious, and spiritual ideas which are a great part of human heritage, but also a non-dogmatic and disciplined process by which seem to our human thought as indispensable to the survival of human race at the present critical juncture of human history and to the eventual development of a greater civilization than we have had hitherto."

During the last four years the government has expressed the urgent need to formulate concrete and practical plans for value oriented education. The high level conference held at Shimla on 27-28th May, 1981 is to be considered as one of the significant events in the history of 'Value Education'. During the two days conference deliberations were mainly centred round on the meaning and scope of value-oriented education and formulating practical guide-lines for governmental action. The conference recommended, inter alia, that value-orientation should be the central focus of education and that teachers should be given the necessary training in the effective methods of development of values among students and teachers. Besides this the conference made many revolutionary recommendations.

In order to undertake a review of the Teacher's Training Programme, particularly with a view to inculcate moral and social values in students, an informal Working Group was constituted under the chairmanship of Shri Kireet Joshi, then Educational Advisor, Ministry of Education and Culture, in May 1981 with the following terms of reference:

i) To suggest the necessary changes in the present content and scope of value-orientation in education with special reference to the need to ensure development and promotion among students and teachers not only of the highest value of physical, emotional, mental, aesthetic, moral and spiritual culture but also of those values which are uniquely Indian, and which would promote secularism, pride in heritage and composite culture.

ii) To suggest a programme of the study of the national

freedom struggle.

iii) To suggest the curriculum content for teacher trainees to achieve the desired value-orientation.

iv) To suggest special techniques of pedagogy for training in value orientation.

v) To suggest strategies for re-orientating serving teachers through in-service programmes.

vi) To suggest ways of promoting participation of voluntary organisations in organising training courses for teachers.

vii) To assess dimensions of efforts required as also to indicate the extent of governmental inputs.

viii) To make suggestions which would be relevant to the determination of the new roles of teachers as counsellors and guides instead of as mere lecturers.

ix) To determine the important tasks that teachers will need to undertake towards preparing the new educational materials keeping in view the challenges of our times.

According to Prof. Venishankar Jha, a noted educationist, "The imperative need of the present time in our country is to create conditions necessary for cultivation of refined professional personality and life-style for the teacher worthy of his personality and dignity as an inspirer and, to no small extent, as a fashioner of human destiny." For the proper professional growth of the teachers the elevation of their social status is very essential. For this purpose, the working group has recommended establishment of a National Council of Teacher Education—very different in scope, and purpose from the existing one. Besides this the working group has made many practical recommendations, which are as under:

1) The curriculum relating to value-education and to the

study of Indian culture should be immediately implemented in all the teacher's training institutions.

2) Until the training institution's are remodelled on new lines as suggested in the report. An interim measure is recommended under which the teacher's training institution should offer three new papers related to and philosophy and psychology of value-oriented education and India and Indian values as optional papers in place of any other three papers which are at present prescribed in the teacher's training programme. In addition, teacher's training institutions may be recommended to incorporate in their total programme of teacher's education as many elements as possible from amongst all the various suggestions that have been made in this report in regard to value orientation.

3) Simultaneously, efforts should be initiated, without delay, to introduce two streams of teacher training programmes (i) five-year teacher-education programmes, after Senior Secondary, leading to master's degree in education and (ii) two-year teacher education programme, after the first three-year graduation of five-year post graduation, leading to master's degree in education. These programmes would be designed on the basis of the pedagogical ideas and value-oriented curriculum suggested in this report.

4) A provision may also be made on an optional basis for the two-year-training programme in such a way that a teacher-trainee could complete the full programme in two phases, the first phase being of one year duration, and the second phase of not more than five-year duration during which the second-year programme could be covered through summer-courses or other short-term courses. Those who have completed the first

year programme could have the possibility of appointment as teachers on probation.

5) Pioneering and pace-setting value-oriented institutions should be established, preferably one in each State, which should be utilised as centres for training teachers on the basis of the new ideas and values recommended in the report.

6) A few national institutes of teacher education should be designed and established, specially to educate the staff of the colleges of teacher education in India.

7) An All India Public Examination for the evaluation of teacher trainees should be instituted, which would have novel features such as the combination of the written test with oral test and submission of a project report: all of which would have a special thrust towards the promotion of excellence, value-education and a sound acquaintance with India and Indian values.

8) Measures should be taken to eliminate various evils and deficiencies which are growing alarmingly in teachers' training institutions.

9) The above recommendations can be effectively implemented if a further proposal is implemented. The proposal is that the Central Government should, by the exercise of its power under concurrency, create a national organisation which would have the following objectives:

   a) To keep under review the institutions and programmes of teacher education in the country at all levels and to maintain high standards of teaching. Research and examination in the field of teacher education with a view to developing attitudes, skills and personality which would reflect the image of the teacher embodied in this report.

b) To establish and to maintain (i) Institute of Teacher Education—designed especially to educate the staff of the colleges of teacher education in India; and (ii) pace-setting model institutions of teacher education, preferably one in each state which should be utilised as centres for training and radiating new ideas and values in the region on the lines recommended in this report.

c) To provide aid, financial, material and human, and advice necessary for coordination and maintenance of high standards of teaching. Examination and research and to stimulate thinking on problems of teacher education.

d) To function as an accrediting authority with powers to recognise or derecognise teacher training institutions and degree awarded by them.

e) To conceive and implement programmes or strategies for bringing the existing teacher education institutions to conform to the aims and objectives laid down by the council.

f) To organise, preparation and publication of variety of resource material including material for audio-visual aids and use of educational technology necessary for promoting high standards of work in teacher training institutions.

g) To organise or support seminars, conferences, symposia as also to set up committees and panels for the promotion of the objectives, functions and activities of the Council.

h) To perform such other functions as may be conducive to the realisation of the aims and objectives of teacher education visualised by the Council on the lines recommended in this report.

10) It is further recommended that the present National Council of Teacher Education may itself be constituted as the above-mention national organisation with this difference in its constitution that it should have, in addition to present composition which consists of Union Minister of Education as President and 40 other members, an executive body consisting of a full time Chairman and five full time members to be appointed by the Central Government, which should have the power to appoint standing committees and other committees for carrying out various functions and responsibilities. The Member Secretary of the Council will also be the Member-Secretary of the executive body. The Chairman and members should be eminent educationists, teachers and educational administrators.

Prospects of Value Based Education

An official committee, under ex-Chief Justice J.S. Verma has produced a 500 page report on it with these words.

The quality of our life is revealed in the virtue of reverence without idolatory. Reverence involves refusal to pay more respect to the lesser than to the greater or to the smaller than to the larger context. It means giving greater reverence to the community of truth and to the ultimate source. The call to reverence always stands in tension with the injunction against idolatry, which continually questions what we give our reverence to. Idolatry involves preferring the familiar over the infinite, the local over the universal, the urgent over the important, the visible over the invisible, the short-term gain over the long-term perspective, treating the former as if they were absolute. Some forms of idolatry are easy to spot. Others are more subtle and so, more dangerous. Modern life and its values have introduced many forms of idolatry into our life and its transactions. These have almost been taken as normal and proper behaviour and attitudes.

The present crisis is global and multidimensional. None of the existing single institutions or religions or systems seem to have a complete answer. That is why a new integral paradigm, a new model that transcends a one-dimensional philosophy and a mechanistic worldview, recreating the unity of all people and indeed of life itself is the imperative need. Science, through relativity and the quantum theory, has brought an organic and inter-dependent worldview, replacing the earlier dualistic and mechanistic perspective of Newton and Descartes. Strange as it may seem to some, the mystics of the twentieth century like Sri Aurobindo, Teilhard de Chardin, Rabindranath Tagore, to name a few, have seen this integral vision of reality.

National Regeneration can come about only through a culture of peace and non-violence, and through an education, founded on the strong spiritual heritage of India. It can come only through a networked response by persons of different religious affiliations, and aimed at establishing global solidarity and world peace. Science and religion are becoming less and less hostile and instead of treading separate and divergent paths, are moving towards a convergence of goals and purposes. Also, in our education for a culture of peace and nonviolence, we have a constitutional command and invitation. We are asked to lay stress not merely on our rights alone, but give equal emphasis on our fundamental duties to the nation, to our fellow citizens and to self. This is what the Constitution of India, under article 51 A spells out as fundamental duties of the Indian citizen. This must be included in the educational curriculum.

Many of us know of a very large number of persons of goodwill who want to do something positive to bring about a change in the status quo. Yet they remain dormant, their voices not raised, their hands not put to action. In any attempt to re-construct our Indian people and rebuild a new Indian ethos, the young have to have an active part. Hence the teachers of the young are critical players in this movement of nation building. Religions in India have also to play a critical and constructive role, through inter-religious dialogue and cooperative joint action. A new Indian renaissance based on the deep religious insights of our land and the perennial wisdom of our people, integrated with the developments of science is the need of the hour. We hope to see a new India, where the people are truly free, love one another, share with one another and enjoy peace and joy of life. Neither the violence (coercion) of Capitalism nor of Communism has redeemed humankind from oppression and dehumanisation. So we need to search for a more relevant alternative.

Would it be correct to say that many of us, if not most of us, experience an absence of peace, both within ourselves and outside us? It is not only the poor and the needy but often also the well-off and the affluent, those with good jobs and enough money in the bank, who experience this state in a pronounced way. Stress, leading to strain and ending in sickness is an all too frequent phenomenon of our modern life. Specifically many experience fear and tension in the prevailing conditions of conflict and violence, whether due to inter-caste hatred, or due to the acute disparity between the rich and the poor or due to the inter-religious divide. In the busy modern life and conditions, and in the cities, we often experience lack of space. In fact, this is true, not only of physical space but also of psychological and personal spiritual space. Side by side, we also feel secluded, isolated and experience the pain of being disconnected, alienated from colleagues, from Nature, from our own heart and from God. We yearn for open and free spaces. We yearn for the touch of others, for community, for relationship, for love. Loveless marriages, unfriendly neighbourhoods and communities, finding ourselves strangers to one another in the big cities, etc.—these are becoming increasingly common. As a result, we experience a great deal of loneliness, And we develop compulsions, prescriptions, resulting in rejections, pushouts and left-outs.

This absence of peace (*shanti*) seems to be true, not only of adults but unfortunately of many young children as well, children at home and in our schools. In our passionate pursuit to maintain strict discipline (done out of goodwill and with good intention, no doubt) children are often suppressed, oppressed, threatened, punished, humiliated and controlled in so many ways that their natural spirit of enquiry, their spontaneity, their sense of wonder and wanting to get involved in direct experience have been severely inhibited. The result is that many children experience an absence of peace and well-being, resulting in tensions and so experience 'death' at an early age. In the conventional classroom, the focus is on the outside, on subjects, on another's vision and not inside, namely that of the teacher or of harmony and cooperation were also emphasised. The report, however, was lost in the maze of political changes. The National Policy on Education, 1986 and 1992 made the following statements on the need for value education.

"The growing concern over the erosion of essential values and an increasing cynicism in society has brought to focus the need for readjustments in the curriculum in order to make education, a forceful tool for the cultivation of social and moral values. In our culturally plural society, education should foster universal and eternal values, oriented towards the unity and integration of our people. Such value education should help eliminate obscurantism, religious fanaticism, violence, superstition and fatalism. Apart from this combative role, value education has a profound positive content, based on our heritage, national and universal goals and perceptions. It should lay primary emphasis on this aspect."

Value education has been one of the favourite topics of all educationists, social reformers, preachers, scholars, saints and savants. Gandhiji identified truth and non-violence as the two pillars for ensuring peace, prosperity, progress and perfection in thought and deed of every individual. To Gandhiji real education consisted of drawing the best out of every individual. To achieve the same what better book can there be than the book of humanity. He goes on to elaborate the ideas on education in various facets in his writings and speeches at various levels.

Mahatma Gandhiji's Perception towards Value Oriented Education

According to Prof. Walia, "To Gandhiji every individual human being was prominently significant and had the capacity to contribute immensely to the society and humanity. He has written extensively on education and his perceptions on what would suit the needs of education in India. To him it was necessary to develop educational models that were rooted to the Indian soil and which derived their strength from the age old traditions and experiences of the past with an eye on the future. Character building was critical in his scheme of things and he could not see how this can be done without religion. He was concerned that we were being reduced to a state in which we were losing what was traditionally and culturally Indian and were not able to acquire the new from the alien system. Character building if not pursued could result in tremendous damage to the socio-cultural fabric of the society. He regarded character formation as the foundation for launching movement and struggles not only against alien rule but also against ignorance, illiteracy and poverty. To him real education did not consist in packing the brain with information, facts and figures or in passing examinations by reading a prescribed number of books but in developing the right character. The explorations and possibilities of non-violence would prove profitless without character."

In his writings Gandhiji had elaborated the educational concepts at several places. Education to him is that which "helps us to know the *atman*, our true self, God and truth. He desired that every branch of knowledge should have as its goal, the knowledge of the self. In the activities which he delineated in his Ashrams, several activities was devised with this aim in view. These to him were true education. When activities are carried out without any reference to the goal of knowledge of the self, they become a means of livelihood but not of education. True education always meant a proper understanding of its meaning—devotion to duty and the spirit of service. It liberates human beings and empowers them to preserve the values and sublime aspects of life.

Essentially, Gandhiji's perception of education focus on moral values and ethics. They highlight the concepts of selfesteem for every individual. He firmly belived in practising what he preached. Essentially education must lead to internalisation of the obligation on the part of each human being to be noble in word, thought and deeds. In a plural society, it should also help the individual to celebrate the plurality and yet visualize inherent unity of values and a life of dedication to others.

Content of Value Based Education

One of the most familiar messages in Indian culture is strive for the betterment of all; the prayer 'let all people live happily in good health and cheer Sarve Bhavantu Sukhinah. Nowhere else has such an evolved essence of the thought processes aimed at the well-being of others concretized before India. Earlier Indian scriptures exhort everyone to serve others. Sacrifice for others and serve mankind. If school children are exposed to such an approach exposed at an early age, it is bound to evoke long lasting impressions which would evolve in course of time as they grow and face the world around them.

In a global scenario of erosion of values, it would be difficult to have individuals in society who would strive to halt the process of value deterioration, unless and until schools produce young person with the right aims and objectives of human life. This should also give a clear indication of what should be the curriculum of education in years to come and how the same could contribute in developing the culture of peace within the communities, amongst religions, countries and eventually, globally.

Education must familiarize the child in the initial stages, with the surroundings, the environment, the beauties of nature, the happenings all around through an understanding of living being in their various forms, stages and settings. Gradually they become familiar with language, mathematics and social and scientific aspects of learning which have to be retained in the present day context. The trend of focussing only on specified examination oriented subject areas needs to be discarded. The focus in education must change towards the making of a person, who would contribute not only with information and knowledge but also with understanding amid insight of the ever evolving processes of human growth and development. Only such a person can fruitfully participate in enhancing the quality of the individual as well as of community life.

Gandhiji's efforts were not limited to the struggle for freedom from British rule. Even an overview of his writings would indicate that he had gone into every aspect of human life at the individual level as well as at the social, community and national levels. Much before Independence, he had his plans ready for an indigenous education system that would familiarize children with their surroundings, their people and then with India as a whole as their own motherland.

School Curriculum and Value Education Programme

According to Prof. J. S. Rajput, (formerly Director NCERT) the curriculum content of school education must be indigenous and within the comprehension of both the teacher and the learner at each stage. The teachers' comprehension should not extend only to transmitting information from a prescribed textbook to the children but in developing capabilities to evolve the curriculum from the surroundings itself at the primary stage of school education. In developing such an approach, the criticality of the need for value inculcation and emphasis on ethical and moral education should form an integral part of each and every unit and activity. Stories from the epics, mythologies and history suitable to the stage and linked to value inculcation would generate interest amongst the young learners and could familiarize them with the cultural evolution and heritage. This would also lead to understanding of the culture and heritage of different communities and gradually help in developing respect for religions, languages and cultural practices which may be different from that being practised and evolved in the learner's own home surroundings.

These are the times not only of universalizing elementary education but also of universalizing science education which along with technology is gradually becoming the basic foundation of all the endeavours of development. Learning of science and technology should aim at developing the scientific temper which would provide rationality and lead to logical interpretation of various issues, occurrences and situations. Learning must lead to social cohesion and a spirit of cooperation and willingness to work in a group. It could also lead to the inculcation of the desire to work with others.

The schools must establish mutuality with the communities in various ways, particularly in nurturing in the children this spirit. Communities and individuals would value education more and more in the future. They would also assess the 'gains' accruing out of education returns they are receiving. A couple of action points could possibly contribute effectively:

- It is necessary to liberate the child from the compulsive chains of prescribed curriculum and give the teacher and the learner freedom to evolve and develop curriculum around their own situation in the initial stages of school education utilising the national guidelines to maintain basic uniformity with pronounced flexibility.
- The hesitation in delineating strategies for value inculcation from religions through its various sources needs to be given up. Efforts to develop a sense of self esteem and pride in being an Indian and in the individual's own capability to respect other religions and their practices must be imbibed thoroughly and thoughtfully.
- A sense of belongingness must be developed in every individual learner by focussing on India's contribution in areas like mathematics, sciences, maritime, medicine, trade, architecture, sculpture, establishment of institutions of learning is emphasized and made known to the learners to develop a sense of belongingness to the nation with respect and an attachment to the past. That would give the child confidence and help him/her towards better performance and achievement in future.
- Teacher preparation must ensure development of commitment amongst teachers.

It is a tough proposition when most of the other sectors are influenced by self interest and material pursuits. However, teacher education needs to emphasise throughout in its programme that teachers alone can kindle the spirit of value based growth and development and motivate others to lead their life with full commitment and adherence to common values as imbibed in the Constitution of India.

With all the limitations, deficiencies and rigidities inherent in our educational system and functioning of the schools and other learning centres, transformation and overhaul of the system can be achieved only through the combined efforts of the teachers and the communities. A value based approach must form the backbone of the educational system as well as the teacher education system. Effective and visible steps need to be taken by the teacher, education institutions and motivated schools at the earliest. The multiplier effects would be tremendous to strive and infuse into the students an intensive desire to become cultured citizens first, and then active pilgrims and illumined, volunteers on the path and in the service of society and the world.

Chapter-V
Strategies for Inculcating Value Education

Introduction

Swami Akhandanand rightly said "The problem of fostering ethical and spiritual values in a society raises the question of the source of these values. It is precisely in this field that sharp differences of opinion have developed in the modern age leading to utter confusion and bewilderment. Broadly speaking, these differences reduce themselves to two view points, one of which holds that matter or outer nature is the focus of all values and the other which affirms man as that focus. The first leads to undue emphasis on the creation, possession, and enjoyment of material wealth and the search for organic satisfactions, whereas the second, while putting due emphasis on the above, leads to the pursuit of values and satisfaction lying beyond the sensate level of life and to the experience by man of spiritual freedom and integrity."

The value-orientation is not confined to those only who are in schools, but also for those who are outside. It is a time-bound process; but it is very long and continuous process. If education is a life-long process, as some educationsits have put it, value-orientation is also to be observed as a life long process. It is more so because it is more informal than education. Moreover, the faculties of mind of an individual take different shapes at different phases of life. Therefore, the principle of 'individual difference' is to be followed more carefully in the context of value-orientation.

Strategies to Inculcate Value Based Education Suggested by Various Commissions and Committees

Advocating the value-based education, the great philosopher Ross said, "Today more and more thoughtful people have come to believe that if we wish to build and maintain high class civilisation and protect it from brutality or savage-conduct after some time, then it is necessary that education should be based on morality." Gandhiji, the father of the nation, supported moral education and said morality, good conduct and religion are synonyms for me. The fundamental principles of morality are equal in all religions. Children must be taught the principles and it should be considered enough religious teaching.

After independence, every commission and committee made efforts for the enrichments moral-values and gave its recommendation that moral values should be included in the curriculum and even mentioned those methods by which moral values and civic-sense may be established. National Education Commission (1964-66) has written, "We believe that moral and value education should be given through both direct and indirect method. We give more importance to the work of indirect effect.

Various commissions and committees have emphasised on both direct and indirect method in this regard.

(A) Direct Method:

(1) Fixed hours in the time table for moral values and civic-sense education.

(2) Citation of moral stories, incidents, traditions, etc. by teachers.

(3) Giving students civic, moral and social value education

through education.

(4) Telling students biographies and autobiographies of great religious and social leaders by the teachers.

(5) Study of moral books, religious books (scriptures), religious controversies and comparative religion by the students.

(6) Discussion on religious and moral issues in class and queries by students.

(7) Teachers should guide students in moral problems of students during sports.

(B) Indirect Method:

(1) *Silent meditation*: If we start work with silent meditation it makes our day full of energy and freshness.

(2) *Morning Assembly*: Prayer and morning assembly occupies the highest place in various school activities and it is the best place of value establishment.

(3) *Religious Celebration*: The anniversaries of religious founders and religious celebration of all religions should be celebrated. Lectures and spiritual instructions on universal principles of various religions should be preached on such occasions.

(4) *Corporate Life of School*: The corporate life of school can be made an important medium of giving religions, specially moral education. Teachers and students and each and every student get a golden opportunity of mutual relationship, and listing and learning moral values.

(5) *Group Work:* Education commission has suggested various type of group work for the development of religious, moral and social values in the education.

(6) *Suggestion and Inspiration*: Religious and moral ideals can not be developed forcibly or by order in the mind

of the children. Teachers should give the suggestion and inspiration to children. University Grants Commission has written 'The best method of suggestion is through personal example, routine life and work. Simply it means practice before preach."

(7) *Atmosphere of School*: The intellectual development of a child is meaningless devoid of moral development. Therefore, he should be morally developed and intellectually as well. This development can not be made through lesson citation. It is possible only when the atmosphere of the school is of such kind that the children get religious strength for his moral progress.

(C) Some Methods for Civic-Sense Development:

(1) Training of traffic rules in school.

(2) Education of good conduct and cleanliness in schools.

(3) Education through routine activities.

(4) The development of civic-sense through exhibition and audio-visual material.

(5) Pictures and sayings of great persons related to cleanliness in the school campus.

Suggestion for Teachers

The teachers will have to keep a watch on their conduct and behaviour. Students do not learn moral values and civic-sense merely from book, but they learn by observing their teachers' behaviour and by hearing them. If the teacher considers "teaching work" just a profession and formality, then how will moral values and civic-sense develop in children. It is widely accepted that children learn emotional virtues by observing their elders' behaviour and by following their foot steps. Willingly or unwillingly a teacher is role model which students have tendency to emulate in their primary stage. It is the prime responsibility of every teacher to present himself amicably and exhibit healthy tendencies, working habits and life styles. The teacher as a person imparts knowledge and expertise but is also innovator of tendencies for children's inner and outer individual behaviour.

- In short, the above can be explained as follows:
- The teacher should watch his words.
- He should watch his action.
- He should watch his character.
- He should watch his heart.

A teacher has an important role in the enrichment of moral values and civic-sense. Therefore, the teacher himself should evaluate values. He should always behave well with the students. He should focus on his own discipline instead of imposing discipline on the students. He should mention values from the syllabus and value based questions should be given as homework. He should not miss chances of reinforcement and create awareness among the student about the utility of values.

Suggestion for Social Science Teachers: The teacher can make the subject interesting by using a lot of audio visual devices. The following methods should be used.

(A) *Story Telling* : Story telling is a very old method. Teaching moral values and value education becomes easier with the help of stories. The teacher can easily make the pupils differentiate between wrong and right. All the children are fond of hearing stories from childhood. Even when they grow up, these stories are ever-fresh in their memories. Story-telling can easily be used in social science teaching. By including the incidentes related to the lives of great heroes of history viz-freedom fighter, renounces's, thinkers etc. moral-values and value education can be enriched.

(B) *Story playing / Role playing*: There is unlimited possibility of role playing in social science. The staging of stories or incidents is helpful in clarifying moral values. The teachers may voluntarily select topics and incidents. These incidents may be presented in classes and child-associations (b*al-sabhas*).

(C) *Biographic Approach*: Biographic approach may be made a part of social science teaching. There is a bulk of teaching of moral-values. *Sarvodharm sadbhav*, co-operation, peace, non violence and cleanliness, punctuality, discipline, dutifulness, etc. can be enriched through biographic approach. A student can observe these values at home also.

Suggestion for Teachers Educators regarding Value Based Education through Inspiration

Inspiration has great importance not only in the field of education, but also in other Discipline. A person can do any work with great ease if he is inspired enough. Good inspiration create aim of achieving high life. Inspiration occupies a very important place in moral values and value education. Ericsson has imagined such a moral society in which all the members are to achieve the preferred values with the help of inspiration alone. Thondike inspires children to remove their faults to attain goals related to development of values. Kohlburg goes even further and lays stress on farsighted behaviour obtained from inspiration. Teachers should treat it as important and use it for the enrichment of moral-values and civic-sense.

The Yashpal Committee (1991) wrote (after going through the guidelines of National Education Policy) that every school should make organised effort to develop the same essential qualities in all the children, which have been discussed further. These are such basic qualities which will contribute to individual, social and emotional development in the long run. Teachers are expected to have all of these qualities.

1) **Regularity and Punctuality:** These values are expressed in praise for importance and value of time and punctuality and on sensitivity. All are aware of their importance in every walk of life. For example, children learn such habits or life-styles which makes regularity and punctuality a part of their natural behaviour's.

2) **Cleanliness:** It refers to that basic tendency which a person learn towards his environment. This tendency finds expression in a child's habit of healthy living and keeping himself and his environment clean. This is another quality; which is directly linked with those learning experiences of the children which are provided to them in school and homes in their early life.

3) **Laboriousness:** It is not as much related to those specific behaviour which children should observe, as much to that values which they link with the attainment of goal through hardwork. The development of these qualities prepare children to take the responsibility of purposeful work, execute them with patience and finish them punctuality.

4) **Dutifulness and feeling of service:** These qualities are expressed in the devotion to sacrifice self-interests for the welfare of other and working without fear or prejudice. It implies the sympathy for neighbours, companions, handicapped, old people, etc. and devotion of providing them help.

5) **Equality:** There should be no discrimination on the ground of caste, creed or sex. This attitude should be confirmed through school experience so that he may grow up to be such an adult who considers himself a part of his own community. Every one among them

has some common rights, responsibilities and duties towards the society. The final goal is to help children in their progress towards a world which is beyond linguistic, cultural, religions, social and other economic differences.

6) **Co-operation:** The value of working together to gain the common goal should be developed in the children by providing them proper opportunities of living and working together in and outside the school. Children should be made to understand mutual dependence of moral, local, national and international level so that they may understand the need for co-operative efforts. Undoubtedly this work should be done with care so that the teaching of self dependence, individualism, competition which are equally important may not be endangered.

7) **Responsibility:** Responsibility in the children refers to the devotion of facing difficulties and problems with commitment and confidence. For it, confidence of positive image of oneself and his individual capabilities should be developed.

8) **Truthfulness:** The basic inspiration to be truthful in one's behaviour in every walk of one's work and life is such a quality which every person must acquire. Truthfulness has wide importance in the determination of a child's behaviour and it makes every person's behaviour valid and verified. It is indispensable to guide children properly in school and at home and to help them to develop will-power to put their thought and behaviour into action (truthfulness). Sense of fear associated with telling the truth is case misdeeds should be done alone away with.

9) **Nationality oneness:** The children should learn to feel oneness with the nation. It should be a long and similar

process which may develop respect and willingness in the children to protect fundamental values established in the constitution and respect for national emblems.

Suggestion for Parents: The community should directly be linked with the moral values and value education. The parents have to perform a democratic role in this context. Just sending their children to school is not parent's responsibility. Family has an equal role in this regard—what do their children learn in schools? What difference is visible in their behaviour? Do they utilise their time or not? What culture should be given to them etc. The great scholar, Socrates statement is quite true, "Family is the first school of good conduct" children learn culture moral-values and civic-sense or behaviour for the first time from the family. The negligence of moral responsibility towards the children is not fair.

Family can play an important role in fulfillment of schools' goals. The main responsibility in the development of moral value and value education is on the shoulder of Parents. Parents should consider the development of moral-values and as their responsibility, pay attention to the following suggestions:

1) Parents should co-operate in the schools' efforts for inculcating moral-values and Value Edu. They should not express negative attitude towards teachers' in front of their children.
2) Help children to understand moral-values, but do not impose their thoughts on them.
3) Parents should not advise their children to follow such values that they themselves are not following. The child may get confused on seeing the difference between words and deeds.
4) Set Value Education related examples so that students

themselves may follow them. Family is the first place of values like good behaviour, cleanliness, discipline etc.

5) If the child talks about values in the context of school or society, then don't make a fun of him rather try to understand the problem and encourage him. Praise him so that he keeps making such efforts at his level.

6) Parents should help children in value-clarification and analysis instead of sermonizing them.

7) If confronted with decline and crisis of moral values and disappearing civic-sense related examples, then discuss with all the members of the family and encourage children for equal participation in such discussions. Keep the psychological state of the children in mind and learn about the development process of children from teachers.

8) The contribution of the grand parents in the enrichment of moral-values and civic-sense in children is very important. It is regretful that the generation gap is increasing continuously. The middle generation i.e. parents should recognise their responsibilities and respect and defense for grand parents should be developed. Parents should be able to ensure their future's security along with mutual benefits at both levels.

9) All the members of the family should make efforts to prevent immoral behaviour happenings in their neighbourhood and society and they should not try to save themselves only.

10) Parents should make every effort to protect children from bad company.

11) Parents should provide their children with value enhancing related literature and discuss them, if

children behave against values for some reasons, then create an atmosphere for discussion instead of scolding, criticism or confrontation.

Need for School-Parent's Co-operation

If school and family work together, such a bridge will develop in which a bright future can be built with mutual co-operation. The co-operation of teachers and parents is necessary for the enrichment of moral values. Proper value education starts from the home and it will develop good character. Children will be able to develop all their capabilities in such atmosphere. This bridge will create good environment Parents Teachers Association (PTA) needs to be made strong.

The Need for Reform in the Overall School Atmosphere

If the school really wishes to develop moral-values and value education then it will have to eradicate their present demerits. Equality, mutual love, and co-operation is essential in the schools' atmosphere. Physical atmosphere also affects the school, for the attainment of moral values' goals. The reality is that the whole school e.g. classes, compound, department, cleanliness, arrangement of drinking-water, toilets, even the walls gives us impression of Value Education. The walls of the schools and their cleanliness are the first impression because any comer may get familiar with the culture and values of the school through their decoration. The picture and the sentences written on the walls reflect the philosophical ideology. The picture and the words in the gallery of the school may develop moral-values and civic-sense. So the school campus should be kept neat and clean. Charts, ideals, statements, maps and pictures should be used wherever necessary. The atmosphere creates strong foundation of value based education.

According to the Yashpal Committee, children learn values like punctuality, faithfulness, cleanliness, service, co-operation etc. informally in the school's atmosphere. So it becomes necessary that these qualities should reflect in the school activities and organisation and maintenance of the system for example, if the school campus is not clean or there is bias among girls and boys in the school activities, then there is very little hance that children will learn the values of cleanliness and equality of the sexes. Thus, maximum attention should be given to organisational structure, and the system of the school so that 'school' may become powerful instrument to help in the development of value of non scholastic field.

Suggestions for the School:

(1) The school should be equipped with proper equipment (material and psychological). Only then can the school be decleared as a good school. It is the basic condition for the development of moral-values and value education.

(2) It would be more beneficial to end double-shift system because the duration of one shift is not more than 5 hours. So the curriculum does not prove successful in such a little time. If the schools that are run only in one pitch ve shift, then moral values and civic-sense may be developed through curricular programmes and activities. Observations proved that the schools that run in double shift are just completing the formalities. In winter, in morning schools, any activities takes place only after 10 a.m. Even the morning assembly has to be postponed due to thick fog. Additional time is spent in teaching; consequently important activities like debate, essay competition, quiz, exhibitions, etc. have to be postponed. The condition of the afternoon shifts is just as bad in the months of July-August. In the

scorching Sun, the afternoon assembly is just a formality. Sweating children can be seen becoming irritable and fainting due to the unbearable heat. It would be better to organise evening assembly instead of afternoon assembly. Efforts should be so made that school may prove helpful in the establishment of moral-values and civic-sense.

(3) Alongwith meditation in the school assembly, percepts related to moral-values should be displayed. Examples from a great person's life should be cited. Such avtivities could be based on recommendations made by various committees regarding moral values.

(4) Eco club should be setup in the school and environment awareness should be created. The saying of great persons should be displayed and education of moral-values and civic-sense should be emphasised on.

(5) The desired goals can be achieved through established N.C.C, N.S.S, Scouts sand Red Cross Societies.

(6) Curricular activities should be directed properly and honestly because students learn more through such activities than through books. If we want to enrich values like brotherhood, living together, co-operation, goodwill, tolerance, non-violence and placeful, co existence and civic-sense like duties of citizens good citizenship, importance of discipline, cleanliness then curricular activities are a permanent stage for it which it must be organised honestly. Such organisation should not be formal but real and creative.

The Need for Reforms in Curricular activities

Curricular activities can work as an important tool for the development of moral-values and civic-sense. The overall school curriculum needs to be reformed alongwith social service. The above mentioned values can be developed by including the following and reforming the above mentioned.

(1) **Prayer Assemblies:** The best place of giving Value education is the prayer assemblies of the school. The need is to reform it. The desired goals can not be obtained with the formality with which the assemblies are being directed. Infact, moral values like discipline, regularity, co-operation, good will, dutifulness, etc. and principles of civic sense can be taught through prayer. Patriotism can be developed in the national anthem. Prayer assemblies of various religions should be organised and the desired goal can be achieved through explanation of their implied values. Inspiring incidents from great persons life and educating stories are cited in the prayer-assemblies. All the students can be inspired by encouraging the student who have got recommendable achievement. Therefore, prayer assemblies can work as an effective medium for inculcating values.

(2) **Sports and Playground:** The activities of the playground affects Value Education a lot. The qualities of co-operation, goodwill and equality can very easily be developed through sport activities. The value of punctuality and equality emerge in the playground so, there should be joyous environment during the sport. The energy of the students shoula be utilised in sports. The degree of neatness and cleanliness of the school environment is an indication of the school's values.

(3) **Student Parliament and School Court:** Justice is an important moral value to run life smoothly. Good people not only demand justice for themselves but also for others. Students should be given the opportunities to create sense of justice realize the value of justice For is youth parliament is a beneficial curricular activity.

Students learn the importance of just life and try to follow justice. In the same way, students committee may be made, for example, decoration committee, cleanliness committee, touring committee and cultural programme direction committee. Students courts can be established for classes and school likewise. The defaulters student's issues can be discussed sspecifying when students will perform a particular task then only will the value explanation process will become strong. Students will bring reform in their behaviour and will be aware of the wrong deed. Students can get opportunities of leading a value-based life by understanding the work of executives in the students council.

(4) **Cultural Programme:** Cultural programme undoubtedly develop good and refined tastes and tell us about our culture. National, historical, social, and religions festivals can be celebrated. Folk-song, dramas, folk dance, tit-bits, comedy, dramas, and folk stories can be performed in such programmes. Anniversaries of great persons can be celebrated. In the same manner, literacy programmes may be staged through seminars, conferences, and competitions etc.

(5) **Cleanliness Campaign:** The students should have the knowledge about cleanliness from school. Personal and environmental cleanliness is a very important value. Students can adopt many a beneficial qualities from it. It produces equality and co-operation. Students can participate in writing and speaking about these aspects in cleanliness weeks. All these activities can be considered civic-sense education's compulsory part.

Group songs play an important role in co-curricular activities. Students get various type of education of character-building by practicing groupsong. Open library programmes can be run. Social science is the only subject that is to perform the basic function of tackling burning problems. Social science can perform the moral of developing moral values related to peace, good-will, love, co-existence, and civic-sense like dutifulness, sacrifice, rules and regulations and discipline in the routine life of the students. The refined tastes which are nurtured from the beginning, become an essential part of the personality, so, curriculum should be made according to the time.

In short we need following changes in the system.

1. The need for social transformation.

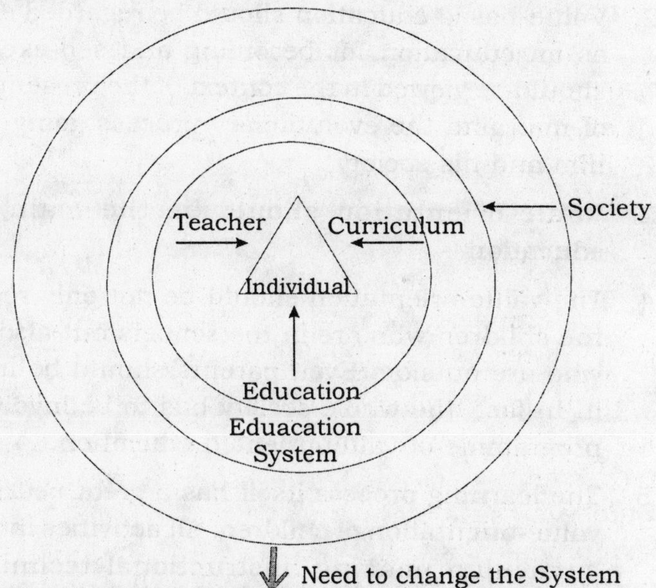

Interdependence of each aspect shown by this picture so we need transformation in each part

2. The need to strengthen the education system.
3. The need to reform curriculum.
4. Teachers: The need to change responsibility and

behaviour.

5. Parents: The need for association with school and interference.

Strategies for Inculcating Moral Values

For inculcation of values and development of character and personality, the report of the High-level Seminar on Moral Education, organised by the Department of Education in the social sciences and humanities of the NCERT at Shimla (May, 27-28, 1981) has given the following recommendations:

1. Provision for value-based education should be made throughout the country with due regard for flexibility of approaches.
2. Value-based education should be regarded essentially as an education for becoming and self-exceeding. It should be viewed in the context of the present situation of man and the evolutionary process going on within him and his society.
3. Value-orientation should be the main focus of education.
4. The value-orientation should be not only required for the children who are in the schools but also for those who are outside. Even parents should be involved in it. In fact, the whole society has to be involved in the programme of value-oriented education.
5. The learning process itself has a great bearing on the value-orientation of children. All activities in the school curriculum making, instructional techniques and evaluation, etc. should be so designed that they lead to the spontaneous development of desirable values.
6. There is a need for producing literature especially designed for the value-orientation for education.
7. All teachers in the schools should be regarded as

teachers of value-education and all subjects including physical education can be used for inculcation of right values.

8. There should be an integrated approach in the value-oriented educational programme. Instead of tackling piece-meal such areas as awareness of ecology, environmental protection, community developmental productivity, population stabilization, aesthetic etc. they should be handled in a comprehensive manner under the board spectrum of social responsibility and inner development of human personality. Concerned ministers of the Government should co-operate with one another in this nation-building task.
9. There should be foundation courses both at the secondary schools and universities aiming at giving the children basic knowledge about India, its people and cultural tradition. The course should also aim at making students feel proud of their country and responsible for its upliftment.
10. Some pilot projects for school improvement should be taken up and the Government of India should constitute a steering committee for this purpose.
11. There is a need for establishing a resource centre for literature on value-oriented education. Besides printed matter this centre should also produce 35 mm films emphasizing desirable values. An effective distribution system for making these materials available in all corners of the country should be developed.
12. Special schools designed for value-oriented education should be established in every state. There should be at least one institution which imparts value-oriented education from nursery to the post-graduate level.
13. Special teacher-orientation programmes should be

taken up at the state level to train teachers in the effective method of development of values among students and teachers.

14. Some case-studies of schools, where value-education is being imparted successfully should be taken up.
15. There should be a national council for discipline consisting of people who would have moral authority in their own right, and who could guide development of value-education programmes. Members of this council could be invited by state educational authorities and other agencies concerned with education for guidance and advice.
16. There should be an education for enforcement of law. A code of conduct for every class of persons should be developed and value-education programmes for the whole society should be so designed that everybody learns to respect the social order.

Report of the University Education Commission (1948-49)

For inculcation of moral values, the Commission suggested introducing silent meditation, study of the lives of great religious preachers and the study of central philosophy of different religions.

Report of the Secondary Education Commision (1952-53)

The Commission observes that healthy trends in regard to religions on moral behaviour spring from three sources:

(i) The influence of the home which is the dominant factor;

(ii) The influence of the school through the conduct and behaviour of the teachers themselves and life in the school community as a whole;

(iii) Influence exercised by the public pupils of the locality and the extent to which public opinion prevails in all matters pertaining to religious or moral codes of conduct. No amount of instructions can supersede or supplant these three essential factors. We, however, feel that such instructions can be supplemented to a limited extent by properly organised instructions given in the schools. One of the methods adopted in some schools is to hold an assembly at the commencement of the day's session with all teachers and pupils present, when a general non-denominational prayer is offered. Moral instruction in the sense of inspiring talks given by suitable persons selected by the headmaster and dwelling on the lives of great personages of all times will help to drive home the lessons of morality. In view of the provision of the constitution of the secular state, religious instructions cannot be given in schools except on a voluntary basis and outside the regular school hours; such instructions should be given to the children of the particular faith and with the consent of the parents and the management concerned. In making this recommendation we wish to emphasis that all unhealthy trends of disunity, rancour, religious hatred and bigotry should be discouraged in schools.

Report of the National Commission on Education (1964-66)

The Commission Recommends

(1) The Central and State Governments should adopt measures to introduce education in moral, social and spiritual values in all institutions under their direct control on the lines recommended by the University Education Commission on religious and moral instruction.

(2) The privately-managed institutions should also be expected to follow suit.

(3) Apart from education such values be should made an integral part of school programme. Generally some periods should be set apart in the timetable for this purpose. They should be taken, not by specially recruited teachers but by general teachers, preferably from different communities, considered suitable for the purpose. It should be one of the important objectives of training institutions to prepare teachers for this.

(4) University Departments in comparative religion should be specially concerned with the ways in which these values can be taught wisely and effectively and should undertake preparation of special literature for use by students and teachers.

Modernization of Curriculum and Text Books

Curriculum in our country is relatively static. As a result it becomes difficult to impart value-oriented education. A mere theoretical exercise does not good to any body. Therefore, the procedures regarding changes in syllabus should be simplified. As a result of which the time lag between the coming of new ideas and their place in the curriculum and their introduction in class will be reduced. The syllabus should contain subjects like our cultural heritage: biographies of the great educators and national heroes, folk-tales drawn from different regions of Indian Union, human geography of region, scientific and industrial development in the past and present languages, religions, national integration, citizenship, harmony among communities etc. The syllabus should be exposed to discussion by a large groups through seminars, so that the interpretation will be more accurate. The teachers should be familiar with the new ideas and instruct the students accordingly. New suitable teaching techniques should be evolved with a view to give value-oriented education. Books should not be produced under commercial motivation. They should be produced on a cooperative basis by a large number of teachers and should be nationalized. These measures will help a lot for the implementation of value-oriented education. (See Tables) on the following pages

VALUE COMPONENT	CONTENTS	TEACHING DEVICE	TEACHING OUTCOMES
TRUTH	Indian heritage Pertaining to truth, all religions of the world i.e Hinduism, Buddhism, Jainism, Islam, Christianity, Taoism, Confucianism, etc Contents of these religions based on truth in the form of prayers, strotas, hymns, stories and messages	Memorization group Singing , story telling, Related charts and Pictures, biographies of Great leaders, visits to places of historical importance	Students will Acquire skills and knowledge. They will learn to respect their own religion and culture and that of others as well. They will show. better tolerance of other faiths. They will Understand unity of Faiths and religion. They will develop a feeling of brotherhood and treat one's father as God.
NONVIOLENCE	Non injury at body and Mental level, seeing oneself in	These content matters can be taught to children through	Feeling of oneness with nature and man, will

VALUE COMPONENT	CONTENTS	TEACHING DEVICE	TEACHING OUTCOMES
NONVIOLENCE	others, extension and expression of love to all human beings, loving God through all of this creations, Universal love as all pervasive a way to moral and spiritual perfection.	Loving flowers, birds, animals, helping plants to grow, practicing tolerance in daily activities, reading stories, poems on Man and God; drawing pictures regarding God's creation	express feeling through poetry songs, drama etc. They will follow non violence in attitude and action
RIGHT CONDUCT	Students need to develop ethical skills, self help skills and social. Skills	These skills can be acquired by the following activities and: Group acting, Monoacting, dramatization, Storytelling., service activities and attitudinal tests.	A child with a balanced, dutiful, disciplined personality. A child having effective leadership skills, and an efficient follower in society.

VALUE COMPONENT	CONTENTS	TEACHING DEVICE	TEACHING OUTCOMES
LOVE	Love for Parents, family members, neighbors, love for creation, and love for all. Service to all as the Motto. Love will lead towards Faith culminating in "Spiritual Love".	Spiritual love can be achieved or can be taught to the pupils by the following devices: Story telling, Dramatization, historical and spiritual trips of places of worships, showing	Students will appreciate truth, feeling of oneness, love of God and his creation and attitude of service to another

Social Values in Education

Individuals constitute society which has certain ideas, models and norms in general in respect of behaviour, conduct, duties and responsibilities towards one another. Love to humanity, universal brotherhood, sincerity, honesty and integrity of character, firm attitude of rendering help and doing actions and works in general benefit etc. are some of the constituents of healthy social life. True education aims at developing individuals into social beings having these virtues.

Schooling is a preparatory stage for cultivating the sense of social values. For example, in the laboratories, where students work in a co-operative way, develop a scientific attitude towards social life. In libraries, while sitting together for self study , they practice patience. In the hostels, students while leading a corporate life imbibe the spirit of living together like brothers, behave harmoniously, sinking their differences and experience what the members of society do for adhesion to human and humane feelings. Activities correlated with academic aspects afford them opportunities for bringing about their physical and intellectual development, strengthening common bonds of spirit. Organizations like N.C.C., N.S.S., Boys Scout and Girls Guide help the students to develop themselves physically, inculcate in them the patriotic virtues and enthuses in them for safety and security of the country at the time we need. Thus, we impart social values to the students in our school systems.

Social values have been emphasised at every stage of social development. The ancient Indian educational institutions attached importance to social values. The students in the *'Gurukulas'* had to render service not only for their students community, rather for the institution as a whole. For instance, they would go to the habitations for collecting meals from worthy householders who took it as their duty to set apart a portion of the cooked meal for the students. Dried fuels they would collect from the forest itself. In medieval times, the system continued. But the occupation of the country by the foreigners a new system of education was ushered in different periods, emphasis was given on Muslim education and western education. Western education aimed at producing, "white-colour *baboos*, to help them to run the administrative machinery of the state. From this period onwards Indian social virtues disappeared from Indian mind and service to the ruler not to the societ stood as the ultimate aim of education."

With the dawn of independence, all this was put in the reverse gear. Education now, has been accepted as "No.1 nation building activity." We have developed a national system of education, to help education for all round development. The achievements so far are not satisfactory. We need to develop social values both inside and outside educational institutions. Students should learn that love for the country means love for the nation, and love for mankind leads to international sympathy.

It paves the way for the formation of education for international understanding, which is the cry of the day for world peace. The social values of education in free India is thus of paramount importance for establishing world peace.

Strategies for Inculcating Social Value

Social values can be inculcated by introducing a programme of educational value of social service. Social servicc implies service to society or groups of individual bound together by rules or conventions or other considerations for achievement of objectives and aims. Therefore the individual has to render service first to himself, bringing about his growth in such a way as to enable him to prove to be of use for the society. He is to prove himself useful as a member of the family, to the neighbours, the state, the country and the world. The educative process has, therefore, to see to it that the development of the individual is consistent with this aim of usefulness and fitness in the objectives and aims in general.

Education is a stage of preparation for cultivating the sense of social service in its theoretical aspect through teaching of lessons dwelling on social virtues and through practicals in laboratories where students work in co-operative way developing scientific attitude and guiding on another under the supervision of experts. The following activities should be undertaken by the schools to impart educational values of social service to the students:

(1) Education at the pre-school stage consists in the upbringing of infants in the home atmosphere. Hence attempts should be made to cultivate virtues of affection, love, truthfulness and obedience at this stage of education.

(2) At the primary stage affection for all, love for the country, truthfulness in behaviour, obedience to elders, curiosity for knowledge, and appreciation of nature outside should be cultivated.

(3) At the Junior High School stage straight forwardness, frankness, uprightness, affection and kindness for all, sense of rendering help to other in times of need should be cultivated. The foundation should be laid for the formation of character and cultivation of qualities of leadership.

(4) At the secondary stage, love for all mankind, preliminary knowledge of different aspects of nature, kindness and help to all living beings, dignity of manual labour, respect for the constitution of the country, sense of maintaining country's independence, freedom of

thought, speech and action in the just and right context and interest for the defence of the country should be cultivated.

(5) At the college and university stages all these virtues should be developed and their practical aspect strengthened.

(6) Programmes of manual labour as cleanliness of neglected localities etc. picnics, excursion etc. be arranged to give opportunities to the students for moving among different people and seeing monumental achievements in the country for broadening outlook and understanding humanitarian values.

(7) Campaigns against disease can be arranged by the students of higher education.

(8) Provisions should be made to educate the deaf, the dumb and the blind etc., and other categories of the disabled.

(9) The schemes for removing illiteracy in general should be undertaken out of love for aid and benefit to mankind.

(10) In order to develop aesthetic sense, training in drawing and painting should be arranged.

(11) Music and dancing are parts of the cultural aspect of social service. Hence, necessary training in this respect should be imparted.

(12) Lady students should be encouraged to organize mass-cooking, mass-knitting of woolen equipments, visit to orphanages, doing voluntary service to orphan children such as pairing off their nails, washing and bathing them.

(13) Students should be engaged in minor construction works like repairing and constructing roads, houses, digging well and tanks etc.

(14) Students should render voluntary service during natural calamities.

5.12 Training of Citizenship

An individual becomes a citizen when he feels he is a part of the community and that he is there to share its burdens. In educational institutions, attempts should be made to give education for citizenship in order to promote the cause of liberty and democracy. Citizens are not born. They are to be trained, therefore, the following strategies should be undertaken in order to develop the idea of citizenship among the students.

(i) Education for citizenship should become a dynamic element in our pattern of education.

(ii) Attempts should be made to inspire the students to develop a sense of cooperation for worthy causes, capacity for critical thought and freedom to place his point of view reasonably.

(iii) Schools should provide activities like debates and discussions on the issue and problems of our country mock parliament, mock *panchayats*, mock-assemblies etc. in order to inculcate proper civic values and attitudes.

(iv) In order to achieve the ends in view, the schools should organize excursions to places of historic, religious and cultural importance.

(v) A student should learn to work in a social context and to come into contact with his fellow men and women in variety of ways in order to achieve his personal desires.

(vi) Every boy and girl should willingly undertake useful productive work, which may be mental or manual. In the process he should not be a burden or a parasite on others and can render some service to society.

(vii) Special camps like N.C.C. or A.C.C., N.S.S., I.V.S.P., (International Voluntary Service for Peace) should be organised to provide a natural environment for the students so that they can develop a sense of commandership which result from free group activities in work and play.

(viii) Students should be encouraged to organise self-Govt. in order to learn the art of dividing different activities amongst themselves intelligently to carry their duties in a disciplined manner and to obey their freely chosen leaders; which are all very essential for good citizenship.

(ix) Teachers should have a good understanding of adolescent psychology and be able to establish sincere and friendly relations among the students.

(x) In order to encourage co-operative group work, schools should organise co-operative societies, where students should actively participate.

(xi) Students should be encouraged to organise pen-friend clubs, on the entire state and inter-district basis.

(xii) The school should celebrate birthdays of great men and woman and of our country like Lord Krishna, Gautam Buddha, Shankar, Gandhi, Gopabandhu, Tagore,etc., Sarojini Naidu, Raj Kumari Amrit Kaur and also the celebration of important days like the Independence Day, the Republic Day etc.

What has been mentioned above is only by way of suggestions. These social services can be motivated by physical, mental, intellectual and spiritual considerations recognising human values and ties of spirit. They are based on social virtues which can be cultivated and developed inside and outside the students learning centres.

Health Values

Good health is a valuable asset to man. It brings for him happiness and prosperity. It is not merely absence of disease. It includes the full development of physical and mental aesthetic and spiritual power of man. Sound health is the greatest blessings of all and is a condition for joyful and energetic life. Therefore, it is very much essential for our students to acquire knowledge of diseases, its causes and prevention of physiology and hygiene. Ignorance of the origin and nature of disease, lamentable lack of hygiene. Knowledge on the part of the student, chronic poverty and cold indifference are responsible for the fall of physical standard of the Indian students. Hence, the centres of learning should impart knowledge of health sense, health attitude and health values. The National physical efficiency tests should be administered on a universal scale to assess the development of health values among the students.

Strategies for Inculcating Health Values

The welfare of the individual and the general good of the society depend largely upon the physical efficiency of our children. It can be materialised by organizing health and cleanliness programme in the schools. In order to make the health and cleanliness programme successful the following programmes should be organised:

(i) Most of the students suffer from malnutrition, enlarged tonsils and adenoids, defective vision, arries of teeth etc. Therefore, medical inspection of the students is absolutely necessary. The actual health conditions of the whole school-going population, their height, weight, nutrition, mental condition etc. must be ascertained and recorded. The school Medical Officer will be able to find out the physical defects which prevent the child from obtaining a full education.

(ii) Teachers should be oriented about hygiene and

practical medicine.

(iii) The Principal should take special accounts of the kinds of sickness which are liable to spread to an epidemic.

(iv) Ample provision should be made for free flow of fresh air and outflow of initiated air. There should be cross ventilation in the classrooms.

(v) For every hundred students there should be 6 closets and 6 urinals. These should not be too near to the classrooms.

(vi) To orient the students about good food habits, picnics should be organised by the schools.

(vii) They should learn how to drink clean water.

(viii) Schools should have first aid box.

(ix) To make the students cheerful and energetic, physical exercises like drill, running games and sports should be organised.

(x) The programmes of '*cleanliness*' may be organised to develop a sense of cleanliness among the students.

(xi) The school Medical Officer should periodically visit the school hostel. He should inspect food and should see that every student eats at regular hours and takes enough outdoor exercise. He should also look at the sanitary conditions of the hostel and its surroundings.

The Recreational Values

'Recreation' refers to both intrinsic and instrumental values. It includes the multifarious programmes organised in schools which give an opportunity to the students for self-expression and self-fulfilment. The laboratories and libraries, play grounds and debating halls have high recreational values. These places of the temple of learning help the students to utilise their leisure house for self-cultivation through various academic, aesthetic and cultural activities. It makes education meaningful and takes care of the entire personality of the young people, their minds, their bodies, their general, moral and spiritual well-being. Hence, a serious and sympathetic attempt should be made to develop recreational values in the centres of learning in our country.

Strategies for Inculcating Recreational Values

Introduction of Work Experience

After Kothari Commission (1964-66) report it was felt that work-experience should be introduced at all levels of education in order to relate education to life. Several Committees and Commissions have been appointed by the Government to bring about a change in the present system. The Ishawarbhai Patel Committee (June-1997) pointed out that "Work experience which was intended to be an integral feature of teaching learning process that followed the introduction of the new pattern." The committee recommended the introduction of SUPW and community service to be introduced in the curriculum. Consequently, in values of dignity of labour can be inculeated in the minds of children.

The SUPW programme should be organised in different schools in collaboration with State Education Department They should conduct orientation work and evaluate the entire programme.

The Aesthetic Values

Aesthetic values are those which provide pleasure and happiness to the individuals. Some philosophers delimit these values only to the artistic works. John Dewey, the pragmatist opines that a child can develop a sense of appreciation of geography and shopwork just like music and painting. He can enjoy beauty in mathematics as well as in poetry. Hence we cannot delimit aesthetic sense only to the fine arts. In spite of these differences, we should bear in mind that aesthetic experiences are vitally composed of feelings on heart and mind.

Little children have aesthetic impulses. They express these impulses through clay molding, finger paintings, paper work etc. thus the aesthetic values develop among the children from their infancy. Therefore, in the school programme, aestetics occupies a very important place.

All possible attempts should be made to make the school a centre of attraction and joy to which children have to flock and not a place of boredom and soul-killing routine work. The school campus should be a thing of beauty that is a joy for ever.

Strategies for Inculcating Aesthetic Values

1. Organization of Cultural Value: To culture and train the emotions and to sublimate the lower human instincts, the school life should be crowded with full-blooded programmes like drama, music, recitations, folk-dances and other cultural activities. It will enable us as teachers and facilitators to discover the talents, organising skill and resourcefulness that we make dormant in the students. Music both vocal and instrumental, gives an opportunity to discover the novelty and originality of our students, develop aesthetic values.
2. Exposure to works of art, beauty in nature, actions of moral worth.
3. Providing situations and opportunities to practise aesthetic values.

Sources of Value Based Education

There are many different sources, which can be utilized

by the teachers to impart value education. They are as follows:

(i) Regular subjects of the school curriculum is the first source of value education. Whatever subject we teach, there is a set of values, which is hidden in structure and methodology. The teacher will have to find it out and accordingly impart instructions. For example, general science is associated with such values as free inquiry, commitment to truth and mathematics is associated with such qualities of mind as logical thinking, neatness and precisions. Similarly, literature and history have their own distinctive values. The correct teaching of the subject, and not only transmission of the information containted in the subject but even more importantly including in the learner, the qualities of mind and heart involved in the pursuit of that discipline. This subject can be used as source of value education.

(ii) Co-curricular activities are the second important source for the development values in school children with its multifarious programmes, which are not only packed with education and instruction, but also provide young pupils with opportunities for self-expression and self-fulfilment, the school should be humming with life and the students should find them attractive and congenial playing fields. Debating halls should be throbbing with life and intense activity throughout the year.

The students-self-government in school, NCC, NSS, Boy Scouts and Girls Guides, Red-Cross, the various clubs and associations, games and sports, excursions and field visits, all provide opportunities for the school goers to come together in the pursuit of common goals and ideals. Besides the development of creativity and distinctive intellectual, social and cultural interests, students also learn from these activities, the values of democratic living co-operation, tolerance, secularism and responsibility. These activities provide experience in learning values through actual living. Therefore, wide participation in school activities should continue under the supervision teachers.

(iii) The school environment is the third source of value education. Some great Hindu personalities in students like Tagore, Gandhi, Sri Aurobindo and Gopalbandhu laid much stress on the creation of a conducive environment in centers of learning for the development of personality of the students. The personal examples and hard work of the teachers, the ideals of the teachers, pupils and the parents help the students to acquire right values in life.

Role of the Teacher in Value based Education

The teacher of the modern day school has to play a very important role in value-oriented education. First he must know that value education is not a sphere of activity distinct from his other professional activities as a teacher. Acquisition of values goes on constantly in the school and outside through many different activities like instruction, relationship with pupils, co-curricular activities etc. Values are also transmitted through general tone of the school and the prescribed syllabus. It is very important for the teacher in the modern school system to develop behaviour in accordance with the highest standards and ethics of their profession. It will help for the creation of a school climate that is conducive to the development of higher values and ideals. A teacher of a modern school should remember the following principles:

(i) He/She should help to create an atmosphere of love, trust and security in the school.

(ii) He/She should have knowledge of child development

and its developmental characteristics and adopt methods accordingly.

(iii) He/She should relate value education to concrete situations, because a young child cannot distinguish between a lie, fantasy and truth.

For example stealing is wrong, does not make sense to a child who has no understanding of the concept of property.

(iv) He/She should organize value education indirectly through different co-curricular activities.

(v) He/She should also impart deliberate value education cautiously.

(vi) Whatever subject he/she teaches in the class, he /she should not deviate from the fact that he is a value educator. The students should be enabled to understand the subject in totality.

(vii) Students are the best judges of their teachers. They judge the personality of the teachers in part but as a whole person. Therefore, the teacher should develop his personality to influence his student.

(viii) It is said, "Example is better than precept". Therefore, whatever values the teacher preaches in the class, he should show it by his own behaviour. A dishonest teacher cannot preach honesty. The teacher should be honest in his dealings with the students. If a teacher of education loves his subject, students will develop love for it. If he is concerned about the environment, his students are likely to be concerned too. If the teacher is conscious about the environmental pollution created by sound, light etc. The students can also be conscious about it. If he is punctual, kind, thoughtful, responsible, his students can also develop such qualities.

(ix) Students should learn not to believe things blindly in custom or tradition. Rather the teacher should develop among them rational deliberation and thought.

In this support we can include the Letter of Amarican president Abraham Lincoln which he has written to his son's teacher.

"My son starts school today. It is all going to be strange and new to him for a while and I wish you treat him gently. It is an adventures that probably include wars, tragedy and sorrow. To live this life will require faith, love and courage. So dear ***Teacher*** *will you please take him by* ***his*** *hand and teach him that for every enemy, there us a friend. He will have to know that all men are not just, that all men are not true. But teach him also that for every scoundrel there is a hero, that for every crooked politician, there is a dedicated leader.*

Teach him if you can that 10 cents earned is of far more value than a dollar found. In school, ***teacher****, it is far more honorable to fail than to cheat. Teach him to learn how to gracefully lose, tough with tough people. Steer him away from envy if you can and teach him the secret of quiet laughter. Teach him if you can-how to laugh when he is sad, teach him there is no shame in tears. Teach him there can be glory in failure and despair in success. Teach him to scoff at cynics.*

Teach him if you work wonders of books, but also give time to ponder the extreme mystery of birds in the sky, bees in the sun and flowers on a green hill. Teach him to have faith in ***his*** *own ideas, even if every one tell him they are wrong. Try to give my son the strength not to follow the crowd when everyone else is doing it. Teach him to listen to every one, but teach him also to filters all that he hears on a screen of truth and take only the good that comes through. Teach him to sell* ***his*** *talents and brains to the highest bidder but never to put a price tag on* ***his*** *heart and soul. Let him have* *the courage to be impatient, let him have the patient to be brave. Teach him to have sublime faith in himself, because then he will always have sublime faith in mankind, in God. This is the order,* ***teacher*** *but see what best you can do. He is such a nice little boy and he is my son".*

Conclusion

It has been realized by all that the present system of education, unfortunately, had rejected the essential value of human aspirations and had made itself a dead mechanism. History of India proves that this great tradition has given us values of '*Satya*', *Ahimsa*', '*Aparigraha*', *Maitri*', '*Kaurana*', '*Prema*', *Satya*', *Tyaga*', etc. but it is a misfortne that our children do not get an opportunity to acquire these values through education. Therefore, the immediate need is to have an integral system of education which would cater to the fourfold values as advocated by the ancient indian philosophers, namely, *Dharma*-righteousness, *Artha*-economic independence, *kamae* motional satisfaction, and *Moksha*-spiritual realization. Besides these, "perhaps the most significant need of the hour is to transform the educational system with a view to cultivating the basic values of humanism, democracy, socialism and secularism."[1] Hence it is the need of the hour to make all possible attempts to inculcate value-oriented education in the centres of learning. The educator, the educational administrator and the people as a whole should support this programme and devote their time, energy and resources to make this education a success."

1. *The Ministry of Education and Social Welfare, Government of India (1972): "Education in the Fifth Five Year Plan, 1974-79."*

Chapter - VI
Co-Curricular Activities and Value Education

Introduction

Through these activities, the qualities of leadership, self-discipline, cooperation, team-work, etc. can be easily developed. New dimensions can be given to the personalities of the students. Planning of these activities is very significant, without which these activities may not bear the fruits. "The wise planning and execution of this programme, moreover, can inculcate wholesome and constructive social attitudes among youth, promote emotional security, develop competence in interpersonal and intergroup relationships so important to growing-up, and at the same time provide immediately healthful and beneficial development of the child and society".

Planning of Activities

While planning these activities, it should be kept in view that the themes selected for various programmes are consistent with our cultural heritage. According to Prof N.K. Gupta, "In a programme of education like this one, the tendency is to overemphasise the 'moral' aspect. Moral or morals should not be stated or pointed out directly but must be left to the audience to infer and understand. While selecting themes for projecting the values we have to select interesting, intelligent and witty anecdotes from the lives of not only saints but scientists, politicians, poets, patriots and kings. There should be no distinction of religion or faith. Often we may find one or two themes from the text prescribed for their study. The dialogue and must be simple. A few examples may be cited. Episodes from the lives of Buddha, Shivaji, Nanak, Kabir, Ramanuja, Thukaram, Jesus, Francis of Assisi, Mohammad."

Individual differences, mental make-up, needs and aspirations of several age-group must be kept in mind while planning these activities, Without which they may not render the desired results. As far as school programme is concerned, various classes may be clubbed in the following way – (See Tables) on the next pages.

Morning Assembly

Morning Assembly has been found to be very good too for clarification and communication of certain values. If it is conducted properly it may prove to be very purposive and fruitful for fostering social, moral and spiritual values. Stress may be given on one or two values per day only. By rotation, contents of short speeches, story-telling, recitation, thought for the day etc. may be changed so that stress on one and the same value is not repeated.

Programme for Morning Assembly should not last fo more than 20 minutes. Within 20 minutes following programmes can be systematically planned an implemented:-

A.	Singing of the prayer	5 minutes
B.	Observance of silence	1 minutes
C.	Students' pledge	3 minutes
D.	Thought for the day	2 minutes
E.	Special programme for the day (by teacher or student/students)	2 minutes

Co- Curricular Activities and Value Education

Group	Classes	Level	Literary Activities	Cultural activities
I	I and II	Primary	Recitation, Nursery Rhymes, storytelling, calligraphy	Action songs, Group Song, puppet show, tables based on Nursery rhymes and fairy tales, fancy dress, Painting, Collage work
II	III, IV And V	Primary	Recitation, Nursery Rhymes of slightly advanced nature, story telling, story writing, calligraphy, preparing speeches on given topics, Maintenance of class and house display boards	Action songs, group Song, Community singing, group dances, school, orchestra, short plays and playlets, mono acting, fancy dress., tableaus, Painting and collage work, *Rangoli* and flower carpeting
III	VI, VII And VIII	Middle	Recitation, Elocution, Debates. Quiz, Watch Word, Antyakshri, Story writing and story telling, Slide and film shows on educational subjects Student Council Activities and Youth Parliament, Exhibitions,	Group Song, Community singing Group and folk dancing School orchestra, School band, Ballets and tableaus, Painting, Rangloi. Flower carpeting, Dramas And

Group	Classes	Level	Literary Activities	Cultural activities
III	VI, VII And VIII	Middle	Club Activities,-Science Club, Humanity Club, and Writers' Club; Maintenance of Class and House Display Boards; Preparing class/ House/ School Magazines/ Newsletters.	short plays , Fetes., Organizing various school and cultural functions; Celebration of school Annual Fay, Parents; Day; Celebrating anniversaries and Days of National and International importance.
IV	IX and X	Secondary	All of the Activities mentioned in Group III level abut at an advanced level; Sports Essay writing, poetry writing contests; presenting papers on given subjects; preparing class/ house school magazines;, Group and panel discussions	All of the Activities mentioned in Group III level abut at an advanced level
V	XI and XII	Sr. Secondary	All of the Activities mentioned in Group III level abut at an advanced level; Sports, Essay writing, poetry writing contests; presenting papers on given subjects; preparing class/house school magazines;, Group and panel discussions	All of the Activities mentioned in Group III level abut at an advanced level

F. Announcements by Principal 4 minutes
and /teacher

G. National Anthem 1minutes
(53 seconds)

The timings mentioned above are just suggestive. It may differ from day to day and also from institution to institution. The true spirit of the Morning Assembly must be maintained and utilized for fostering different values. Under the special programme any one of the following activities may be chosen for the day:-

1. A talk by teacher/student on any topic pertaining to environmental studies, religion, morals, values etc.
2. A talk by teacher/student on any topic related to science, current affairs etc.
3. Reading of excerpts from biographies orautobiographies of great leaders, saints, literatures, scientists etc.
4. Group song/Action song on national or patriotic theme.
5. A talk by teacher/student on sports.
6. Recitation of any good poem or story-telling in English, Hindi or Sanskrit.
7. Community-singing.

Out of the six items mentioned above one may be scheduled for each school day. The importance of the messages conveyed by song, thought or excerpt from biography/autobiography must be explained to the students so that they may imbibe it. Similarly silence for a minute or two should be practiced daily in the Morning Assembly for helping pupils in concentration and introspection. Songs selected for community-singing must be in different Indian languages so that pupils may learn to appreciate each other's language. It will be a step towards inculcation of national outlook among them.

The sanctity and dignity of the Morning Assembly should be maintained both by teachers and students and all must participate in it. Eg: If teachers show disrespect to the National anthem, students are likely to follow suit. While presenting the daily programme due representation should be given to Hindi and English languages, boys and girls, senior and junior students. Looking into psychological differences and different needs of primary and secondary children, it is suggested that separate Morning Assemblies for primary sections and secondary sections be arranged. This will facilitate the smooth and fruitful communication between the teachers and students. It may also help to remove dullness to a large extent.

Chapter - VII
Summary of the Book

The problem of modern education is basically the problem of enrichment of moral-value and proper Value Education. The present book is an effort in this direction. Modern life's greatest problem is the decline of moral value and disappearing civic-sense. In the rapidly changing environment, where man has conquered the height of the space and the depth of the sea, progress in every walk of life has been made undoubtedly, but the negative aspect of progress is cut-throat competition, violence, malice, indifference towards values in life and environment.

After independence, essential social, moral and spiritual values and virtues have been declining continuously for the last five decades. Malice and bitterness has increased at all levels. Though it is true that school not untouched from the indifference towards atmosphere and disrespect for values has grown, their effective role and responsibility of the school to give direction to the people of the nation cannot be undermined. Value-based education will co-operate in fighting evils like all types of fanaticism, malice, violence, fatism, dishonesty, corruption, exploitation and drug addiction.

It is therefore essential that moral values and civic-sense and school education's entire programme should be started from the primary phase of school education as an important part of school routine. The curriculum of social science has an important function in this regard. Social science can very well play the role of concern and association towards the society. But at present the whole curriculum is not being properly executed and proper moral-values and principle of civic-sense have not been included in the syllabus. The ten centred constituents of the National Education Policy, 1986, should be popularized. These constituents are:

(1) the history of Indian freedom struggle,

(2) constitutional duties,

(3) essential subject matter to strengthen national image,

(4) India's common culture heritage,

(5) equalitarianism,

(6) democracy and secularism, (Sexual Equality)

(7) man-woman equality, (Sexual Equality)

(8) environmental protection,

(9) the adoption of small family norm

(10) development of scientific outlook.

Fundamental duties which have been given in part **IV** of the Indian Constitution.

(1) To abide by the constitution and respect its ideals and institution, the National flag and National Anthem;

(2) To cherish and follow the noble ideals which inspired our national struggle for freedom.

(3) To uphold and protect the sovereignty, unity and integrity of India;

(4) To protect the country and render national service when called upon to do so.

(5) To promote harmony and spirit of common brotherhood amongst all the people of India.

(6) To value and preserve the rich heritage of our composite culture.

(7) To protect and improve the natural environment including forest, lakes, rivers, and wild life, and to have compassion for living creatures;

(8) To develop the scientific temper, humanism and the spirit of inquiry and reform.

(9) To safeguard public property and to adjure violence.

(10) To strive towards excellence in all sphere of individual and collective activity so that the nation constantly rises to higher levels of endeavour and achievement.

It is necessary to include these constituents properly in the curriculum. The uniform nature of social science curriculum will have to be strengthened in this context so that it may not split into various streams and make the subject burdensome. Rather the concept of 'frugal in words, fathomless in meaning' should be followed in the curriculum. It means that the syllabus of social science should be detailed but it should not be loaded with unnecessary details.

One of the important implication of the present book is to demarcate the role of the teacher. The whole world is under the panic of terrorism, violence, communalism and hostility, malice, amity, co-operation. In the words of Dr. Kireet Joshi we can say "education is a sub-system of culture, and since culture is again a sub-system of the totality of social life, value-education cannot be promoted in isolation from the totality of public life. Unless, therefore, public life (which is at present degenerated not only morally and spiritually, but even in terms of civil life, and in terms of evils of increasing mechanization,) is cleansed, value-education will always be looked upon as something utopian, unrealistic and impracticable."

Again, the cause of value-education can be greatly promoted, if media consents to honour the theme of value education and make a deliberate effort to utilise its services for the promotion of value-based education.

We may now concentrate on our present system of education and consider how, if at all, it can sub serve the purposes of value-based education.

It is evident that in our present system of education, we are greatly removed from the ideals that are implied in value education. In our present system, we are too occupied with the mental development, and that, too, a narrow aspect of mental development so that only those qualities of the mind are attempted to be developed which are relevant to subject-oriented, book-oriented and examination-oriented system. We stress the powers of memory rather than the powers of understanding; we emphasis the power of knowing facts and hardly attempt to the development of the power of imagination. Our process of education is a pursuit of piecemeal assimilation of information, and holistic vision of things is hardly given any place.

Can we do anything worthwhile in the present system? The first answer to this question is that at least the preliminary things can be done even in the present system, provided that one important condition is fulfilled. If teachers consent to change their attitude, then much can be done, irrespective of the system in which we are obliged to work today. If teachers can change their attitudes towards students, they will make a great effort to observe their students with increasing psychological understanding and sympathy. A good teacher can always empathise with the children in the class as a good gardener can empathise with flowers in the garden, whatever their state of development. If teachers look upon their work as sacred work, a work of priesthood, a work of a trustee, a work in which his or her own soul gets directly related to the inmost souls of the children, if teachers perform their tasks with fresh sight fresh vigour, and fresh approach, they can make a great contribution to their children's value oriented integral development. No system prevents a teacher from utilizing the important methods of education such as those of setting an example of high character and providing stimulating atmosphere in the class room for their own students. No system prevents teachers from cultivating powers of expression and powers of explanation, nobody prevents teachers from devoting their own time to the preparation of lessons for the children, nobody prevents teachers from establishing right relationships with children so that they can be inspired to put their trust in their teachers and follow their guidance. There are, indeed, counteracting influences at work, at home in school or in society at large. But still, a good teacher can make a great difference, and in spite of limiting conditions in which they are working, they can still achieve something that is of basic importance.

Parents can also contribute a great deal. They, too, can become good teachers; they can learn how to look after children and learn how to inspire them to develop right habits, right manners and right attitudes towards things and people, towards environment, towards their work, towards their books and time-tables, towards their time of play and time of study. Parents can supplement teacher's tasks in many ways; and parents can also create in their homes value-oriented atmosphere. They can so organise the home life that nothing is displayed in children's atmosphere which is injurious to children's value education. They can also learn how to sacrifice their outer pleasures for the sake of the growth of their children.

It is true that the circumstances in which the families run these days, the tasks that are expected of the parents may not be so easy to implement. There is a big factor of television today in every home and nobody has control over it. This influences our children in a very big way and often in a disastrous way. But, here again, parents' associations can play a great role. They can create a movement in the country to combat this menace. They can pressurise the government to change the policy in such a way that at least the official channels are freed from vulgarity, cheap entertainment, and vulgar advertisements which stimulate lower desires and impulses. They can also create public opinion whereby parents choose the channels for children and ensure that good films and right episodes are witnessed by children. When there is a downpour, you cannot stop the rain, but you can certainly have an umbrella to protect the body. In the same way, when there is a down pour of films on TV, good, bad and indifferent, parents can provide umbrella for their children by means of counseling, and by means of setting certain standards in the atmosphere of the home.

The educational administrators also can help a great deal even in the present system of education. Principals, inspectors, directors and policy makers can ensure that funds are allocated for right purposes, that programmes are so designed, both curricular and co-curricular, that value education and integral education get utmost importance, that atmosphere of the institutions is so designed and developed that in every nook and corner, children find display of beautiful things, inspiring thoughts and ennobling stimulation.

Similarly students also can play their own role. Students can be taught or they can learn on their own how to discipline themselves; they can be stimulated, both internally and externally, how to utilise immense freedom which is available to them in the present day societal environment. They can think of the art of self-discipline, the art of control, the art of concentration. They can also seek guidance of teachers and others as to how to study, what to study and how to develop their faculties, and how to harmonise and integrate their personality.

Changes in the attitudes of the teachers, parents, educational administrators and students can create a suitable climate in which greater reforms in education can be proposed more effectively and fruitfully. For even if there is a new system of education, and the attitudes remain the same, that new system will either not work at all or will become a kind of ornament which might hurt rather than help.

At the same time, it is for the organisers and leaders of education, to think about an ideal system of education and create fields of experimentation so that eventually a new system of education can be invented and implemented.

In this connection, perhaps the most important thing that we need for implementing value education in public and private schools, universities and other educational institutions is to underline the programes of training of teachers.

Making of a teacher differs significantly from making, say, of an advocate or a surgeon. The teacher is more than a mere skilled performer in a branch of his profession. It is true, indeed, that he must have the best of skill in accustoming the pupil to the austere joy of mastering a difficult theme, be it quadratic equation or the equation of E-MC2 or any other similar theme. But in the end, when the frontiers of knowledge change, the importance and even the validity of what is learnt may not survive. What survives is the discipline of learning and the values acquired in the process. Whatever be the topic teacher teaches, the ultimate values of his professional endeavour bear on the habits of lifting and thinking and feeling, the art of life on what the pupil comes to love and care for. Thus the teacher fashions the life of the pupil which is the single theme of all of education. Skills in teaching are, no doubt important, but they do not take the teacher far. An otherwise an unashamedly desolate teacher may teach effectively; he also influences lives of the pupils no less, but sadly. Therefore, a teacher must not only be efficient, but he or she should also be a good and evolved person. The most effective weapon of a teacher is the silent power of example; it matters in the end and always. It is, therefore, necessary that teacher education should aim not merely at cultivation of skills but in making a personality of high character and noble vision. This consideration brings to teacher education a very different purpose and responsibility which are not equally relevant to other professions.

It is for this reason that both pre-service and in-service programmes of teacher education need to be re-oriented in such a way that they provide orientation towards value education.

It is unfortunate that we have still not developed a model programme of value education. This is one of the most urgent needs in order to make implementation of value education practicable and expeditious. The model programme of value education should be so flexibly framed that it can be varied according to the needs of teachers and students or according to special situations that may obtain at any given point of time. There should, therefore, be what may be called a core programme. Core Programme of value education should have an:

1. Intellectual dimension
2. Aesthetic dimension
3. Ethical dimension

These three dimensions should again be related to an

over-arching or all-comprehensive umbrella of spiritual education.

A very important part of this programme should be devoted to the theme of science and values, considering that the modern civilization is undergoing an unprecedented crisis because science and values have been divorced from each other. They need to be brought together in a happy harmony if we are to deal with the crisis effectively and fruitfully. The programme should also have practical aspects which may involve exercises of volition, exercises of aspiration and exercises of introspection. There should also be opportunities where students can participate in works of community service or situations where courage and heroism can be developed. It is not sufficiently realised how much physical culture can contribute to the practice of values. An ideal sports person develops more easily the qualities of courage, hardihood, energetic action, initiative, steadiness of will, rapid decision and action, perception of what is to be done in an emergency and dexterity in doing it. An ideal sports person embodies the true sporting spirit, which includes good humour and tolerance and consideration for a right attitude and friendliness to competitors and rivals, self-control and scrupulous observance of the laws of the games, fair play and avoidance of the use of foul means, equal acceptance of victory or defeat without bad humour, and loyal acceptance of the decisions of the appointed judge, umpire or referee. Above all, an ideal sports person develops the habit of discipline, obedience, order, team spirit and cooperation. While speaking of these qualities that physical culture can contribute, Sri Aurobindo has written:

"If these could be made more common not only in the life of the individual but in the national life and in the international where the present day the opposite tendencies have become too rampant, existence in this troubled world of ours would be smoother and might open to a greater chance of concord and amity of which it stands very much in need. The nation which possesses them in the highest degree is likely to be strongest for victory, success and greatness, but also for the contribution it can make towards the bringing about the unity and more harmonious order towards which we look as our hope for humanity's future."

While preparing the proposed programme, we should lay a stress on the right type of teaching-learning material. Here, the importance of stories, plays and passages of literature need to be underlined. These selections should possess qualities of chiseled expressions and refined tastes. Even examples of poetic excellence need to be included. They will help us in emphasizing that just as there is beauty and harmony of physical forms, even so there is beauty in harmony of thoughts and words and rhythms.

Value education is directly related to integral education. In integral education, every domain gets related to its own proper value system. In the domain of physical education, the values that are promoted are those of health, grace and beauty. In the domain of vital education, the values that are promoted are those of harmony and friendliness, of courage and heroism, of endurance and perseverance. In the domain of mental development, the values that are pursued are those of utmost impartiality, dispassionate search of the truth, of calm and silence, and of the widest possible synthesis. The values pertaining to the aesthetic development would be those of beauty and creative joy. The integrating psychic and spiritual development emphasises the value of intimate sympathy for all, mutuality, ever-increasing wideness, process of self-exceeding and attainment of oneness.

Let us also note that integral education admits integrity of life, and invites life itself to be the teacher of the life of the pupil. As life work is through atmosphere and environment created by activities of interrelationship of individuals and things, therefore, integral education aims at creating the right atmosphere and the right environment which are so skillfully organised that outer instruction plays a minor role and personal example of the teacher and nearness of the teacher to the soul of the student play a major role.

It is in this context that a great deal of effort needs to be made to change the atmosphere of schools and universities. So if we want knowledge based and value based society we must introspect ourselves and must take right action at the right time.

Bibliography

Alfred North Whitehead, *Adventures of Ideals*, Penguin books 1948.

A.N. Whitehead, *Aims of Education.*

Clarke, Jay. *Beginning Values Clarification*, Pennant Press, 1975.

Cochrane, Don. *Moral Education – A Prolegomenon*, "Theory into Practice", October 1975, 14, 236 – 46.

Dewey, John, *Moral Principles in Education*, Philosophical Library, New York, 1959.

Dewey, John. *Human Nature and Conduct.* New York: Holt, 1922.

Dewey, John. *Art as Experience.* New York: Minton, Balch, 1934.

Dewey, John. *Theory of Valuation.* Chicago: University of Chicago Press, 1939.

E, Westermark, *The Origin & Development of Moral Ideas*, Vol.II Educational Policies Commission, U.S.A.

Edger Faure, Ed., *Learning to be – The World of Education Today and Tomorrow*, UNESCO Report, Paris, 1972.

Encyclopaedia of Religion and Ethics, Edited by James Hastings, T & T Clark, Edinburg, 1965.

Fraenkel, Jack R. *Teaching About Values.* In values of the

American Heritage: Challenges Case Studies, and Teaching Strategies, Yearbook of the National Council for the Social Studies, 1976.

Friedenberg, Edgar Z. *The Vanishing Adolescent.* Boston: Boston Press, 1959.

G.N. Kaul, *Values & Education in Independent India.*

Harmin, M., H. Kirschenbaum, and S.B. Simon. *Clarifying Values Through Subject Matter.* Minneapolis: Winston Press, 1973.

J. Maurus, *How to Use Your Complexes.*

J. Maurus, *How to Win Personal Efficiency, Better Yourself.*

Kirschenbaum, Howard. *Values Clarification: An advance Hand-book for Trainers and Teachers.* La Jolla, Calif,: University Associates Press, 1977.

Kohlberg, Lawrence. "*The Cognitive – Developmental Approach to Moral Education*" Phi Delta Kappan, June 1975, 56 (10), 670-77.

Kohlberg, Lawrence, "*The Relationship of Moral Education to the Broader Field of Values Education,*" In J. Meyer, B. Burnham, & J. Cholvat (Eds.), Values Education: Theory, Practice, Problems and Prospects. Waterloo, Ontario: Wilfred Laurier University Press, 1975.

M.K. Gandhi, *My Religion,* Navajeevan Publishing House Ahmedabad.

M.K. Gandhi, *Self-restraint* V. Self-indulgence NPH, Ahmedabad.

M.L. Sharma, *Who Is At Fault.*

Metcalf, Lawrence E.,ed. Values Education: Rationale, Strategies, and Procedures. Washington, D.C. National Council for the Social Studies, 1971. pp. 1-28.

N.L. Gupta, *Current Trends & Problems of Progressive Education*, Krishna Bros., Ajmer, 1985.

Osman, J. "*The Use of Selected Value Clarifying Strategies in Health Education, Journal of School Health*, 1974, 43 (10), 621 – 23.

Peck, Robert F. and Robert J. Havighurst. *The Psychology of Character Development*, New York: John Wiley & Sons, 1960.

Rechard B. Gregg, A. *Compass for Civilization*, N.P.H. Ahmedabad.

Rokeach, Milton, "*Toward a Philosophy of Value Education* J. Meyer, B. Burnham, J. Cholvat (Eds.), Values Education: Theory, Practice, Problems, ad Prospects, Waterloo, Ontario: Wilfred Laurier University Press, 1975.

R.C. Sharma, *School Management*, New Delhi.

R.K. Mukherjee, *Ancient Indian Education.*

Rene Wellek and Austin Warren, *Theory of Literature* Richard E. Gross, Walter E. Mephie, and Jack R. Fraenkel, International, Edited, *Teaching the Social Studies*, Text book Company, Scranton, Pennsulvania, 1969.

Shiv Swamy Iyer, *Evolution of Hindu Moral Ideals.*

Swami Ranganathanand, *Eternal Values for a Changing Society*, BVB, Bombay, 1971.

Sears, P.S. and V.S. Sherman, *In Pursuit of Self-Esteem.* Belmont. Calif: Wedsworth Publishing, 1964.

Simon, Sidney B. Leland W., Howe, and Howard Kirschenbaum. *Values Clarification: A Handbook of Practical Strategies of Teachers and Students*, New York: Hart Publishing, 1972.

S.K. Maitra, T*he Ethics of Hindus*, II Edition.

Smith B.C., *Values Clarification in Drug Education: A Comparative Study*", Journal of Drug Education, 1973, 3 (4), 369-76.

Superka, Douglas P., Christine Ahrens, Judith E. Hedstrom, with Luther J. Ford and Patricia L. Johnson. Values Education Source-book, Boulder, Colo: Social Science Education Consortium, 1976.

S. Harman, *Plight of Pupils in Schools,* DL Publication, London' 70.

V.S. Agrawala, *Studies in Indian Art,* Varanasi.

Vinaytosh Bhattacharya, Cultural Heritage of India.

Willis H. Griffin and Udai Pareek, *Process of Planned Change in Education,* Somaiya Publications Pvt. Ltd., Bombay, 1970.

Constitution of India.

Gandhi, M.K. (1956). *Character and Nation Building.* Ahmedabad: Navjivan Publishing House, 2-18.

NCERT (2000).*National Curriculum Framework for School Education.* Delhi, 18-19, 34-36.

Ramamurti, et. Al. (1990) *Report of the Committee for Review of National Policy on Education,* 1986. New Delhi, ix, 19-20,22-23,276-277.

RIMSE (1999). *Value Education: An Outline.* Mysore, 3-9.

Singh, Karan. (1996).*Education for the Global Society.* In UNESCO (1996), learning the Treasure Within. Paris, 226-227.

UNESCO (1996). *Learning the Treasure Within.* Paris, 50,60,91-92.

UNESCO (1980). *Goals and Theories of Education in Asia*: Report of Regional Workshop. Bangkok: UNESCO Regional Office for Education in Asia and Oceania, 6.

UNESCO (2000). World Education Report 2000: *The Right to Education* - Towards Education for all Throughout Life Paris, 27, 93.

University News.43 (08) February 21-27 2005. Article of Prof. A. K. Singh. Prof. and Head, CLS University.

Journal on value education (April-2004) Published by NCERT

WCEFA (1990). World Declaration on Education For All and Framework for Action to Meet Basic Learning Needs. New York: UNICEF House, 2-3.

Anchor of the child's educational and emotional growth.

Sanskrit & Hindi

Ashtadash Upnishad, Edited – Limaya and Wadekar, Vedic Samshodhan Mandal, Pune, 1958.

Bhartiya Niti Ka Vikas, Dr. Rajbali Pandey, Bihar Rastra Bhasha Parishad, Patna.

Charka Samhita, Chaukhamba Vidya Bhawan, Varanasi

Jain – Bauddha Shikshan Paddhati, Dr. N.L. Gupta, Hindi Marathi Prakashan, Sitabuldi, Nagpur, 1985.

Mahabharat Kaleen Shiksha, Dr. N.L. Gupta, Chetna Prakashan, New Shukrawari, Nagpur, 1976.

Manu Smriti, Edited by Hargovind Shastri, Chaukhamba, Varanasi, 1970.

Prachen Bharat Ke Aacharya Aur Unki Uplabdhiyan, Dr. N.L. Gupta, Chetna Prakashan, Nagpur, 1978.

The Mahabharata, BORI, Pune, Udyogparvan and Shantiparvan.

Bhartiya Nitishastra Ka Itihas, Dr. Bhikhaulal Atreya.

Sanskriti Ke Char Addhyaya, Ramdhari Singh, 'Dinkar'.

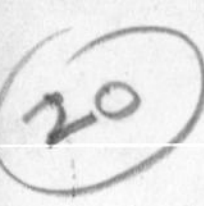